1 CORINTHIANS

Sean Green

PRESS
87 London Street, Reading, RG1 4QA
Email: churchoffice@readingfamilychurch.org.uk
Telephone: 0118 933 7961

Published by Reading Family Church

First published 2017

ISBN-13: 978-1546493471
ISBN-10: 1546493476

Written for my beloved three children.

Printed for my beloved church family.

ACKNOWLEDGEMENTS

I had no idea how much work was required to take several of my handwritten journals and turn them into this study guide. For that to happen a number of people have helped me, and I want to thank them:

Jonathan Davis and the other trustees for encouraging me to make this available more widely, not just for my children.

Karen Fisher for making sense of my handwritten journals and typing them up with a smile.

Dr Nicola Abram for reading every word, editing my prose and asking good questions to bring clarity.

Andy and Kathryn Twine for the final proofreading, ensuring no , . " or ' was out of place.

Josh John for encouraging me while he figured out layout, artwork, publication and logistics.

My fellow elders for trusting me to publish my thoughts on difficult verses without their sign-off.

My wife, Liz, and our three children: Joshua, Lucy and Zoë. You bring the best out of me.

CONTENTS

INTRODUCTION

Paul's first letter to the church in Corinth has long piqued my interest. It paints a picture of a young, zealous church who live messy lives in a complex city. It only takes a few chapters to see parallel issues in the town we live in, and the church we're part of.

The content for this book came from my morning devotions over 18 months. My method was simple: to copy out a single verse, pray for the Spirit to illuminate it, and then write until a page of my journal was filled. This allowed me to see each verse within the context and the flow of the letter. My aim was to grasp what Paul wanted his original readers to understand.

During my devotions I deliberately avoided using other reference material or commentaries. It's not that they aren't helpful, but I wanted first to interact with the Scripture myself.

Having captured my own thoughts, I can now weigh them against other writers with the integrity of having done my homework. And now others can read my reflections, along-side those of learned commentators, as you study the letter for yourselves.

The content for this guide was originally written for my three children, as part of my legacy to them. It is only being published because I was encouraged to do so by the trustees of RFC, as part of my sabbatical in summer 2016. It was never intended to be a definitive statement of what the elders of RFC believe. If you want to know what my fellow elders make of each verse, you will have to ask them.

We all have much to learn from the first letter to the church in Corinth. My hope is that this study guide will help my three children, and all of us at RFC, to be recipients of grace: to be enriched in every way, and not lacking any spiritual gift.

CORINTH IN PAUL'S TIME

The ancient city of Corinth was located at the bottom of Greece, on an isthmus: a narrow piece of land connecting two larger areas across an expanse of water that otherwise separates them.

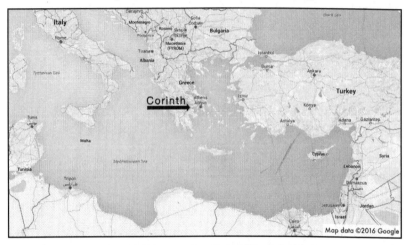

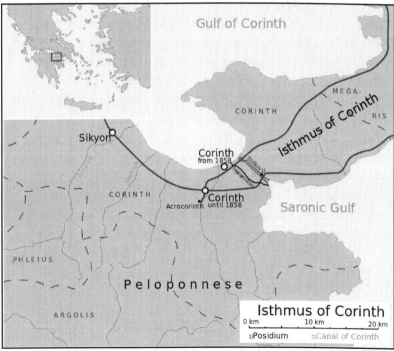

On this isthmus was a huge rock outcrop called the Acrocorinth. This outcrop had a reliable water spring, creating the perfect location for an easily defendable fortress. This security helped it become the crossroads of the western Mediterranean, and it flourished as a settlement.

At that time Rome was the centre of a huge empire, driving a flow of goods and people along the eastern Mediterranean coast from northern Africa to the capital city. The prevailing winds swept down from the boot of Italy, making the journey difficult and dangerous. It was soon realised that it would be better to drag ships and cargo across the isthmus at Corinth, saving time and reducing the risk of shipwreck.

The portage of ships and cargo across the four-mile isthmus meant travellers were in transit for a few days. As a result, the hospitality industry and trading flourished. As these industries grew, even more migrant workers were attracted to Corinth from the Mediterranean basin.

This influx of people brought an influx of lifestyles, preferences and religions. Corinth in Paul's day was a cosmopolitan, socially liberal, religiously tolerant, sexually immoral, thriving sea port.

The city hosted many religions, with their associated temples and practices, as well as the goods and services required to support these various forms of worship.

Most famous among these was Aphrodite, the goddess of love; worship at her temple was expressed through ritual sex. It is rumoured that a thousand sacred prostitutes worked at her temple. The phrase 'to Corinthianise' was coined, meaning to live a promiscuous life.

Corinth also hosted the huge 'Isthmian games', a sporting competition second only to the Olympics. This had been held biannually since 582BC. During the games the demand for accommodation from tourists created a boom for the tent making and repair businesses.

When this context is understood, it makes sense of some of the issues covered in Paul's letter. Because Corinth was a staging post for travellers many apostles passed through the city, and their differing emphases would be felt in the church.

Sex workers are to be expected in seaports, but the shrine prostitutes at Aphrodite's temple made it common to see sex as a form of worship. Corinth's cosmopolitan nature resulted in an abundance of religious practices, including animal sacrifices. This in turn created thriving markets and food canteens, with meat supplied from the temple sacrifices. Greek culture valued and enjoyed new ideas, especially when delivered using spectacular oratory gifts.

This was the Corinth that Paul visited in the spring of AD52, as recorded in Acts 18. Here he met fellow tentmakers Aquila and Priscilla, believers from Rome, and they formed a partnership to financially support their gospel endeavours. Most likely their tent-making and repairing served the needs of the tourists and spectators for the Games. Paul stayed in Corinth for 18 months before moving on, and left behind him a thriving church.

After a few years, news from the church reached Paul while he was in Ephesus. The report was not good. There were divisions in the church. They quarrelled about which apostle to follow: Paul, Apollos, Cephas or Christ (1v12). There was sexual immorality among them that didn't even occur amongst pagans: a man was sleeping with his father's wife (5v2) and the church was proud of this! They had disagreements that resulted in ongoing lawsuits against one another (6v7).

They were using shrine prostitutes (presumably at the temple of Aphrodite) yet were unsure about the role of sex within marriage (7v3). They were confused about whether they could buy and eat meat sacrificed to idols, or what to do should their unbelieving friends invite them to dinner (10v25-30).

Their church gatherings had no sense of order or honour. They didn't wait for each other during communion: some people were getting drunk, whilst others went hungry and were humiliated (11v21).

In fact, their meetings did more harm than good (11v17) However, regardless of all their moral, relational and theological failings, Paul was confident they would be sustained to the end, found blameless on the day of the Lord Jesus Christ.

And what was the basis of Paul's confidence? It was because God - who had called them into the fellowship of his Son, Jesus Christ - is faithful (1v9). The Corinthians may not have been faithful, but God is. Because of His benevolence they did not lack any spiritual gift; they had been given all they needed.

Yes, they were sexually immoral, argumentative, divisive, chaotic and confused - yet Paul wanted them to know that they would be sustained to the end (1v8). They will be found guiltless in the day of the Lord Jesus Christ. That is scandalous. That is grace.

CHAPTER 1

1:1 | *"Paul, called to be an apostle of Christ Jesus by the will of God, and our brother Sosthenes."*

Paul writes from the city of Ephesus (located in modern day Turkey), probably near the end of his three year stay there (Acts 19). He greets the Corinthians by reminding them of his apostleship: a key theme of the letter. This is not because he was insecure, but because he was called by Jesus to this task. Apostles were gifts to churches from the ascended Christ (Eph 4v11). These special representatives established and governed the embryonic church, through their preaching, their delegates, and the letters they circulated. Some of these letters were clearly inspired by the Holy Spirit, and were later collated in what we now call the New Testament. Paul was not one of the original twelve apostles; he was called by Jesus on the road to Damascus (Acts 9).

The only other reference to Sosthenes in the New Testament is in Acts 18v17, when Paul was in Corinth. Sosthenes, the ruler of the synagogue, was beaten by the Jews because Paul's ministry was taking hold. It seems that he came to faith and joined Paul on his missionary endeavours.

> ## *"They have been drawn into the Big Story of what God is doing in history."*

1:2 | *"To the church of God in Corinth, to those sanctified in Christ Jesus and called to be his holy people, together with all those everywhere who call on the name of our Lord Jesus Christ—their Lord and ours:"*

Sanctified means to have been made holy, set apart as sacred, purified or set free from sin. Paul reminds the Corinthians that God took the initiative and sanctified them through their faith in His Son. They are now a holy people - not by chance or by their own desires, but by the will of God. But more than that, they have been drawn into the Big Story of what God is doing in history. Countless others throughout history and their known world were also calling on His name. The Corinthians' voices now join this vast family of worshippers. All have been sanctified through faith in Christ. They are part of a much bigger holy people: the church of God. Paul reminds them of the unity they have with all who follow Jesus, in every place. They are called by God and unified because of Christ; these are strong themes in this letter.

1:3

"Grace and peace to you from God our Father and the Lord Jesus Christ."

Here, then, is the good news that Paul stewards for the Gentiles: unearned favour and wellbeing is theirs (and ours) from God the Father through faith in His Son. Unmerited favour and wholeness comes only through the person of Jesus. Paul opens his letter with this kernel of the Gospel. It's his headline greeting! Peace is more than the absence of conflict but echoes the Old Testament concept of "shalom", where a person's life is in ordered harmony with God and others. Both physically and spiritually, "all is well". The phrase "Grace and Peace" captures the wonder of intimacy and closeness with a holy and transcendent God; it speaks of a favour that produces sublime wellbeing. The source of this blessing is our Heavenly Father; the means of this blessing is Jesus our Lord. This grace and peace cascades through Christ into the hearts of the men and women of the Church of God in Corinth.

> *"They are evidence that Greco-Roman culture is being invaded by the grace of God."*

1:4

"I always thank my God for you because of his grace given you in Christ Jesus."

Paul thanks God for the grace given to the Corinthian believers. He cannot thank God for their "faith", as he could the church in Rome (Rom 1v8). Neither can he honour their "partnership in the gospel", as he could to those at Philippi (Phil 1v5). He cannot thank God for their "faith and love", as he could for the church at Colosse (Col 1v4). Neither can he give thanks for their "faith, love and hope", as he could to those in Thessalonica (Thess 1v3). The best he can do is to offer thanks for "the grace given them". This is not meant as a compliment. The Corinthians had received a great deal of grace, yet their response to that grace was deeply flawed. Their church was characterised by internal arguments, lawsuits, sexual immorality, and drunkenness, and their meetings did more harm than good. Despite this, Paul thanks God for them. The Father has lavished unmerited favour upon them, calling them to believe in His Son, Christ Jesus. Paul reflects upon this, and reminds them of his gratitude. They are evidence that Greco-Roman culture is being invaded by the grace of God.

1:5-6

"For in him you have been enriched in every way — with all kinds of speech and with all knowledge — God thus confirming our testimony about Christ among you."

Paul proclaimed Christ to the Corinthians, and they responded in faith. One of the many outcomes of this transaction - with which we can be overly familiar - is that they were then enriched in every way. They didn't deserve it, but that's who God is. They were supplied with something greater than mere wealth or status: they received a transformation of heart and mind. As a result, they are abundantly supplied to live in right standing before God. They are new creations; the Holy Spirit dwells within them. God has given them value and significance; He has adorned them with His love and mercy. All this is found only in Christ. And this was not without effect upon their lives; their knowledge and speech has changed (as we read in Matthew's gospel, "out of the heart the mouth speaks" – Matt 15v18). Now when they think and speak it is full of life and wisdom - or, at least, it should have been. Paul considers this as confirmation that the Gospel has taken root and is established in them.

1:7

"Therefore you do not lack any spiritual gift as you eagerly wait for our Lord Jesus Christ to be revealed."

This community have all that they need as they wait for Christ's return; they are equipped to wait expectantly for His second coming. Whilst we often think of the Spirit's work as bringing vitality to our lives, too often we overlook the Spirit's gifts as a means of eagerly waiting. The Spirit's activity in the perseverance of the saints is as vital as His work of sanctification of the saints. God's people receive grace both to start and to finish their race. We have all been enriched in every way; we are not lacking any spiritual gift. Jesus has been revealed as the promised Saviour, and will be revealed as the returning King of Kings and Lord of Lords (Rev 19v16). Whilst the timing is unknown, the return is certain, and all who trust in His name are equipped to eagerly wait for that day.

"The Spirit's activity in the perseverance of the saints is as vital as His work of sanctification of the saints."

1:8

"He will also keep you firm to the end, so that you will be blameless on the day of our Lord Jesus Christ."

Not only is Jesus "the judge who is to come", but He is also the one who will sustain His followers until His return. Jesus will keep all who are His strong in their faith. There will be no condemnation for those who are in Christ Jesus. They will be "guiltless" (Rom 8v1), set free from the Law of Sin and Death. They have already been justified through faith (Rom 5v1), so no-one will be able to bring any charge against God's elect. It is God who justifies (Rom 8v33). And on that day of reckoning, Christ's work of keeping us in his hands will be proved sufficient (John 10v28). Paul wants to ensure that the Corinthians are confident of God's saving grace, even though their collective lifestyle and behaviour did not always match their status before God. Paul assures them that God the Father will be faithful on the coming day of judgement.

1:9

"God is faithful, who has called you into fellowship with his Son, Jesus Christ our Lord."

Paul could have simply reminded the Corinthians that God is faithful and that God is true to His vows and promises; that He is able and thorough in delivering on them; that He is steady, constant and keeps His Word. That would be encouragement enough. Yet Paul goes beyond this, and links God's faithfulness to His calling them into fellowship with His Son. They have been beckoned by God into a relationship with His beloved Son. They have been drawn into a sweet communion, sharing companionship with Jesus Christ. They can now expect an 'up close and personal' friendship with the One who has been given all authority over all things. Jesus is infinitely superior, yet the Father has called them into fellowship with Him. Oh, how the riches of the Gospel should warm our hearts!

> *"Oh, how the riches of the Gospel should warm our hearts!"*

1:10

"I appeal to you, brothers and sisters, in the name of our Lord Jesus Christ, that all of you agree with one another in what you say and that there be no divisions among you, but that you be perfectly united in mind and thought."

Given Paul's opening thanksgiving for the church in Corinth, you would think that they were super Christians. He states they are enriched in every way, not lacking any spiritual gift (v5, 7). And yet once his greeting is, he appeals to them to agree with one another. Here, then, is the paradox of the gospel: believers are holy and sanctified, yet still a 'work in progress'. Paul has to appeal to his readers from the highest authority, Jesus, lest they miss the seriousness of this. The Church - who are God's people, Jesus' body on earth and his future bride - are to be "perfectly united in mind and thought". This does not mean that they are to be facsimiles of each other, but rather that they should live and work in harmony, acting as a single body. Just as many instruments combine to make a rich and beautiful sound, so God's people are to act in concert, directed by Christ Jesus.

> *"Here, then, is the paradox of the gospel; believers are holy and sanctified, yet still a 'work in progress'."*

1:11

"My brothers and sisters, some from Chloe's household have informed me that there are quarrels among you."

Paul prepares the ground for his rebuke, and it is worth noting the relational tone of his language: "my brothers and sisters". Paul is known to many of them: he was the founding father of the church (4v15), and he spent at least 18 months amongst them (Acts 18v11). So this is not someone from HQ bringing correction to just another church on a list. Rather, it is a concerned brother intimately involving himself. Note that he lets them know the source of his insight: "some from Chloe's household". Paul names her, presumably to demonstrate the authenticity of the report and to remind them of his close association with them. He wants them to end their quarrelling, but also to understand the root issues behind their lack of unity. Division among God's people is the first thing Paul addresses. He appeals to them from his highest authority, Jesus: the true head of the household they all belong to.

1:12

"What I mean is this: One of you says, 'I follow Paul'; another, 'I follow Apollos'; another, 'I follow Cephas'; still another, 'I follow Christ.'"

The church in Corinth was divided into certain factions, depending on people's preferred apostle or who was baptised by whom (v14-17). Apollos was a Jew from Alexandria; he was a learned man, with a thorough knowledge of the Scriptures. He spoke with great fervour and taught about Jesus accurately. He's first mentioned in the New Testament when he travels to Ephesus to preach (Acts 18v24-25). It was there that Priscilla and Aquila helped him to understand the way of God more accurately. He moved on, but eventually made his way to Corinth - just as Paul took the road to Ephesus (Acts 19v1). Cephas is the Aramaic equivalent of "Peter", and refers to the Apostle Peter. Paul mentions Cephas in his letter to the Galatians, calling him a "pillar of the church" (Gal 2v9). Paul disagreed with Cephas in Antioch, and opposed him to his face (Gal 2v11). Christ is the chief Apostle - and thankfully a few in Corinth had realised this!

> *"Pride divides people and raises up smaller kingdoms."*

1:13

"Is Christ divided? Was Paul crucified for you? Were you baptised in the name of Paul?"

The head of the church is Christ, and His body is not to be divided. The apostles, His sent ones, are merely ambassadors: they are not the king. They are meant to faithfully represent the greater authority. Paul addresses the Corinthian factions by minimising his own importance when compared to Jesus. Paul was not crucified for them, nor were they baptised into Paul's name. The root of the church's division is most probably pride, expressed in misguided loyalty. Pride says "my apostle is better, my experience has greater significance, and my spirituality is richer". Pride falsely elevates and always divides. Pride produces ever smaller kingdoms. Pride has a thousand faces and draws a thousand lines of division.

1:14-15

> "I thank God that I did not baptise any of you except Crispus and Gaius, so no one can say that you were baptised in my name."

Baptism was part of the rallying cry of the factions, presumably because it was a public symbol of accepting and identifying with a teacher. It is a way of outwardly showing that you agree, align and are obedient to someone's instruction. And yet the intention of Apollos, Cephas and Paul was always to point their followers to the true and greater Teacher: Jesus. Paul is not hoping to build his own rabbinic school or Pauline empire. He is reminding them that he did not join them to himself but to Christ; in that sense he has no claims on them nor they on him. They are not his followers, nor is he their head. He answers his own question of verse 13 with a resounding "NO". He is thankful he did not baptise many at Corinth. Paul uses his apostolic authority to lessen his status in their eyes!

1:16

> "(Yes, I also baptised the household of Stephanas; beyond that, I don't remember if I baptised anyone else.)"

We can see here that this letter is being dictated, in real time; first, Paul states that he only baptised two people, then he remembers that he also baptised the household of Stephanas. He also concedes that his memory may be failing him. This is a rebuke with a personal and vulnerable approach. He knows members of their church, they know him, and he admits his mistakes. Acts 16v33 records another household coming to faith and being baptised. The Philippian Jailer was filled with joy because he and his entire household had come to believe. The pattern is set in Philippi and repeated with Stephanas' household - who, incidentally, were the first converts in Corinth and the peninsula region (16v15). That a whole household came to faith and was baptised implies parents, children, and slaves - all who take shelter with Stephanas. This may seem strange to us, given our individualistic culture and personal response theology. Yet we must be open to other cultures and family dynamics, and recognise the Spirit's work of regeneration and salvation in different societies.

> "Paul uses his apostolic authority to lessen his status in their eyes."

1:17

> *"For Christ did not send me to baptise, but to preach the gospel—not with wisdom and eloquence, lest the cross of Christ be emptied of its power."*

Sacraments are religious practices of particular importance and significance. The sacrament of baptism was instituted by Jesus to publicly show entry into His Kingdom. Paul's role was not to gather people to himself, but to proclaim the way to Christ. He was a herald, that Christ may be known and many may enter His Kingdom. He did not bring attention to himself, with a flurry of wise words. Rather, he let the glory, wisdom and offence of the gospel reveal who Jesus is. Apostles are like doormen, opening the way to Christ's expansive kingdom; they have no interest in ushering believers into a grubby concierge office. While baptism is an important response to their message, it was no more than that. Apollos, Cephas and Paul were all ambassadors, heralds and doormen for Christ.

"Paul's role was not to gather people to himself, but to proclaim the way to Christ."

1:18

> *"For the message of the cross is foolishness to those who are perishing, but to us who are being saved it is the power of God."*

Paul wants to move the church's conversations away from the activities of the messengers (Cephas, Apollos, Paul) and encourage them to focus on the content of the message. The cross speaks of reconciliation and unity, by the most unlikely and surprising of means. It is a message of vertical reconciliation between God and those made in His image. And it is a message of horizontal reconciliation between men and women of every class, ethnicity and political persuasion. It is a message of unity based on another's perfection, of strength through weakness, of victory through death, of freedom through suffering, of peace through sacrifice, and of justice through substitution. This type of wisdom is foolish to humankind, but powerful to those being saved. The divisions at Corinth were masking God's wisdom. People were perishing while they were disagreeing. Paul's remedy is a long, hard look at the cross of Christ. All believers throughout all the ages need to be reminded of the gospel.

1:19

> *"For it is written: "I will destroy the wisdom of the wise; the intelligence of the intelligent I will frustrate.""*

God is not averse to exposing our folly. Paul draws here from Isaiah 29v14, where the context is God warning those who "honour me with their lips but their hearts are far from me; their worship is made up only of rules taught by men" (Isa 29v13). Men and women set themselves up against God, thinking that their own wisdom and intelligence can prevail. Yet God will actively come against such thinking; He will frustrate it and tear it down. The cross will affront and assault the wisdom of the "wise". Babel's tower teaches us a timeless lesson: men and women want to build towers for their own glory, but God will tear them down. Paul is reminding the Corinthians of an old plot line: human wisdom will falter. In contrast to this human wisdom, Cephas, Paul and Apollos faithfully proclaim Gospel truth. This is the power of God for salvation, though many will discount it as foolish.

1:20

> *"Where is the wise person? Where is the teacher of the law? Where is the philosopher of this age? Has not God made foolish the wisdom of the world?"*

The Corinthian culture had a high view of the Orator, the Academic and the Sophist - or teacher of philosophy and rhetoric. Paul sets these champions against the wisdom of God. Their best efforts at explaining the world's beauty and torment will always fall short. It is not that their minds are deficient, exactly; rather, it is because they are finite. In contrast to the infinite, eternal, all knowing mind of God, theirs are understandably limited, unilluminated and puny. The Creator can reveal or hide, elevate or demote. The Creator's wisdom has breadth, depth, length and time; it sees the beginning from the end. The Creator's wisdom gives richness to each thread of history; it embraces both the individual life and the collective story. God's wisdoms plumbs both the horror of sin and the glory of Christ. His infinite wisdom makes our best efforts look foolish. Yet there is no shame in the uneven match - unless the created wants to be the Creator.

> *"In contrast to the infinite, eternal, all knowing mind of God, theirs are understandably limited, unilluminated and puny."*

1:21

> *"For since in the wisdom of God the world through its wisdom did not know him, God was pleased through the foolishness of what was preached to save those who believe."*

God the Father knows the inevitable trajectory of human wisdom: pride and ever further estrangement. Yet He did not leave us to the deserved outcome of our wisdom. He decided to use what we consider to be foolish things to both shame the wise and save the foolish. The foolishness of innocent substitutionary death is the power of God for salvation. When the gospel is proclaimed to the wise they only hear ignominy in death on a cross; they only hear failure. And so they perish, along with their wisdom. But when women and men humble themselves and believe the foolish message of the cross, they are saved. Those who believed this foolish preaching pleased God. In effect, they chose to trust God despite how things looked. As the writer to the Hebrews tells us, "Without faith it is impossible to please God" (Heb 11v6).

1:22-23

> *"Jews demand signs and Greeks look for wisdom, but we preach Christ crucified: a stumbling block to Jews and foolishness to Gentiles,"*

Torah-believing Jews wanted their good news of salvation to be validated by the miraculous. They had been taught that the Messiah would heal the deaf and open the eyes of the blind (Luke 7v22, Isa 29v18). In contrast, the Greeks esteemed thought and wisdom - so if the good news of salvation sounded more like "foolishness" it was not going to get much traction. But Paul did not pander to Jews who demanded miraculous signs to validate his message. Neither did he use eloquent words to meet the expectations of his Greek hearers. He simply preached Christ: the stumbling block of Jeremiah 6v21 and the foolishness of sacrificial death. Ironically, the Jews had been given miraculous signs, by Jesus himself, but still they would not believe (John 12v37). Miraculous signs in themselves are not enough; Christ crucified needs to be proclaimed as the way to salvation, in any and every culture.

> *"When humble women and men humble themselves and believe the foolish message of the cross of Christ, they are saved."*

1:24 | *"but to those whom God has called, both Jews and Greeks, Christ the power of God and the wisdom of God."*

It is God who takes the initiative, not us; He calls and we respond. Worldviews or cultural expectations cannot thwart the call of God on someone's life. He opens blind eyes and deaf ears. He softens proud hearts and illuminates dark minds. When God calls, stumbling blocks are removed and the cross is revealed as sublime wisdom. When God calls and Christ is preached, the power and wisdom of God are revealed and applied. Colossians 2v3 tells us "that in Christ are hidden all the treasures of wisdom and knowledge". The power of God is able to transform the weakness of the cross into the defining moment of a glorious plan of redemption. Nothing is too hard for Him. In the crucifixion, the wisdom of God is displayed: God is both Just and the Justifier. This is sublime wisdom on display.

> *"God is both Just and the Justifier. This is sublime wisdom on display."*

1:25 | *"For the foolishness of God is wiser than human wisdom, and the weakness of God is stronger than human strength."*

Paul is not arguing that God is foolish or weak. Rather, the contrast is to illustrate the vast gulf between our 'very best wisdom when on tip-toes' and the steady perfection of God. To be clear, Paul is not suggesting God has occasional 'off' days. Rather he is saying that the Corinthians' 'best' days still fall immeasurably short of God's unchanging perfection in all things. Human wisdom and strength can seem impressive, and certainly there is much of it to celebrate and acknowledge. But our finite minds and abilities, though God given, cannot surpass or even get close to the mind of God. These are words of comfort and assurance, because God is good and full of grace. The God who has enriched the Corinthians in every way (v5), saving them through His 'foolishness', is stronger and wiser than all of mankind has ever been or will ever be.

1:26

"Brothers and sisters, think of what you were when you were called. Not many of you were wise by human standards; not many were influential; not many were of noble birth."

Paul encourages the Corinthians to stop and remember their own circumstances when they were first called by God. Very few of them were educated like Crispus and Sosthenes, the synagogue rulers (Acts 18v8,17; 1v1). While all have been enriched in every way (1v5), few were well connected in Corinthian civil or commercial life. They were much like everyone else: normal people, without much merit in themselves. No doubt some had more material wealth than others (11v22), but few could be ranked as wise, influential, or of noble birth. When God calls people to be His own, He has little regard for education, wisdom, background or circumstance. What matters is not 'what you were' when you were called, but 'who He is' that calls you. It does the soul good to be reminded that God set His love upon us independent of our circumstances or social standing.

> *"What matters is not 'what you were', when called, but 'who He is' that calls you."*

1:27

"But God chose the foolish things of the world to shame the wise; God chose the weak things of the world to shame the strong."

What could be more foolish than a King entering his kingdom in obscurity and poverty? Or choosing the ambiguity and shame of a virgin birth? What could be more foolish than dismissing the crowds when your popularity rises? Or to allow yourself to be knowingly betrayed, arrested - or even executed? What is more foolish than appearing to "mere women" as the first witnesses to your resurrection? Or reinstating the impetuous friend who denied you three times? Or calling and empowering uneducated men and women to further your kingdom? What could be more foolish than appearing to your followers for just forty days? What is more foolish than allowing your people be persecuted and scattered?

Yet it was with the weak and foolish people that God the Son chose to dwell. He gathered them, loved them, commissioned them, sent them and prayed for them. He still does.

1:28-29

"God chose the lowly things of this world and the despised things—and the things that are not—to nullify the things that are, so that no one may boast before him."

God had chosen these Corinthian believers not because they were influential but because He delights in lifting up the downtrodden and reversing desperate situations. He still does. He delights in bringing good news to the poor, binding up the brokenhearted, proclaiming liberty to captives and opening the prison of those who are bound (Isaiah 61). His intention is to demonstrate His glory, and in so doing He removes all grounds for human boasting. He chose the low and despised things to display His sublime wisdom and strength. And yet these foolish things were more than objects by which to display His glory. They - we - are made in His image, and beloved, adopted and sanctified by His Son. Once they - we - were not a people, now they - we - are called to be holy by the will of God (1v2).

1:30-31

"It is because of him that you are in Christ Jesus, who has become for us wisdom from God—that is, our righteousness, holiness and redemption. Therefore, as it is written: 'Let the one who boasts boast in the Lord.'"

In His wisdom, God the Father is both Just and the Justifier. Men and women were made to be hidden in His beloved Son, and attributed with Christ's righteousness. The preaching of Paul, Cephas and Apollos merely heralded this astonishing demonstration of wisdom. Christ became the wisdom that humanity desperately needed. Christ is the means to our robust and enduring righteousness. He is also the agent of our sanctification: by him we are being transformed from one degree of glory to another (2Cor 3v18). But there is more: Christ is also the provision for our redemption. By His shed blood we were purchased out of our enslavement to Sin, Satan and Death. The Corinthians' boast was not to be rooted in the Apostle who baptised them, nor in their worldly influence, wisdom or family of birth. Their confidence was to be in God alone.

"Christ is also the provision for our redemption. By His shed blood we were purchased out of our enslavement to Sin, Satan and Death."

CHAPTER 2

2:1 | *"And so it was with me, brothers and sisters. When I came to you, I did not come with eloquence or human wisdom as I proclaimed to you the testimony about God."*

Paul has already stated that not many of the Corinthians were wise, influential, or of noble birth. In the same vein of thinking, he now reminds them of how he first preached the gospel to them (1v17). He did not use the smooth words or an articulate vocabulary that were the custom of the day. His addresses were not remarkable for their incredible insight or wisdom. Neither did he have a charismatic personality that arrested and held their attention. In fact, some said that "in person he was unimpressive and his speaking amounts to nothing" (2 Cor 10v10). He was simply obedient to his calling, which was to proclaim the testimony about God. His preaching was not eloquent, yet his calling made it effective. When the testimony about God is faithfully proclaimed, what is important should not be critiquing its style but responding to its message.

> *"His preaching was not eloquent, yet his calling made it effective."*

2:2 | *"For I resolved to know nothing while I was with you except Jesus Christ and him crucified."*

Paul did not come to Corinth confident in his oratory skills or powers of reasoning. Nor did he have a suite of popular messages that the crowds would want to hear. He limited himself to the foolish message of the cross - and to be fair to the Corinthian audience, a victory message focussed on death does sound unappealing. His preaching strategy was simply to focus repeatedly on Christ and him crucified. He resolved not to be drawn into discussing local issues, religious disagreements or even his own qualifications as an educated itinerant preacher. He did not want anything to get in the way of his message of good news, and neither would he place his confidence in anything other than this message. He emptied himself of all other concerns, talents and ambitions. He was consumed by, was a single supplier of, and was a one trick pony for, Jesus Christ and him crucified. Paul made sure that his main thing became their main thing.

2:3

> *"I came to you in weakness with great fear and trembling."*

Paul, the great apostle of Christ Jesus, came to the Corinthians in weakness, fear and trembling. Acts 18 describes his first visit, and records the resistance he received from the Jews when he preached in their synagogue. His reasoning didn't penetrate their hard hearts, and the Jews became abusive towards him... Eventually he "shook out his clothes in protest against them" (Acts 18v6). Paul must have felt afraid in these moments, because when the Lord spoke in a vision he said: "Do not be afraid; keep on speaking, do not be silent". Eventually the Jews took Paul to court claiming he was persuading people to worship God in ways contrary to the law. But the case was dismissed (Acts 18v13). This outcome so enraged the Jews that they beat their own synagogue ruler, Sosthenes (we know this as the letter to the Corinthians was from both Paul and Sosthenes). Paul stayed in Corinth for 18 months, and presumably faced ongoing opposition as well his own fears. Weakness, fear and much trembling were all part of his calling. Paul's fears were well founded.

> ## *"Weakness, fear and much trembling were all part of Paul's calling."*

2:4-5

> *"My message and my preaching were not with wise and persuasive words, but with a demonstration of the Spirit's power, so that your faith might not rest on human wisdom, but on God's power."*

Here, then, lies the root of Paul's confidence to forgo eloquence and impressive argument. He did not have superior wisdom or experience, but his teaching was endorsed by a demonstration of the Spirit's power. What form this took is not apparent. It seems unnecessary to reduce it merely to the inner, hidden working of the Spirit changing hearts and giving saving faith - however miraculous and powerful that is. The demonstration of God's power would include wonders such as the lame walking, people being delivered from unclean spirits, violent earthquakes, and healings (Acts 14v10, 16v18, 16v26, 28v8). It wasn't well-crafted messages that authenticated Paul's preaching, but God's power. We can only guess what might happen if preachers spent as much time stirring their own faith for the miraculous as they do crafting words for wise and persuasive sermons.

2:6

"We do, however, speak a message of wisdom among the mature, but not the wisdom of this age or of the rulers of this age, who are coming to nothing."

In Paul's mind there were two forms of wisdom: the world's and God's. The wisdom of the age, or the wisdom of the world's rulers, has to do with the values and priorities of the prevailing culture. That could mean the Greco-Roman culture of first-century Corinth, or the coffee-loving, wifi-hungry culture of the people of Reading today. The wisdom of an age is pervasive; it seeps into all areas of personal and public life and is often expressed without us knowing it. Often, if not always, it is at odds with the wisdom of the mature - that is, those who know God, who have progressed beyond being infants in Christ (3v1). Knowing the Greeks' love for wisdom, Paul explicitly states that the wisdom of the age and its rulers will come to nothing. The "mature" that Paul refers to here have left behind the immature ways of the age and its rulers. As they act upon Paul's message of wisdom, so they continue to grow in Christian maturity.

2:7

"No, we declare God's wisdom, a mystery that has been hidden and that God destined for our glory before time began."

In contrast to the wisdom of the age, which comes to nothing, God's secret wisdom will bring glory in the fullness of time. This secret, hidden wisdom from God was centred on Christ. This wisdom was weaved into the story of the human race, from the garden promise of a serpent crusher (Gen 3v15) right through to the One at the end of this age declaring "I am making everything new" (Rev 21v5). All of this, and everything in between, was purposed in eternity past. The Jewish people were stewards of this secret: they had been given the Law and the Prophets. Yet they did not grasp its vast breadth nor true glory as they searched the scriptures (John 5v39). God's wisdom is displayed through the story of our salvation, "for he chose us in Christ before the creation of the world to be holy and blameless in his sight" (Eph 1v4). This wisdom will continue to be outworked until "the kingdom of the world has become the kingdom of our Lord and of his Christ, and he will reign forever and ever" (Rev 11v15).

> *"This secret, hidden wisdom is from God and was centred on Christ"*

2:8

> *"None of the rulers of this age understood it, for if they had, they would not have crucified the Lord of glory."*

At first glance, it seems that Paul is excusing the rulers of their actions: they didn't realise that Jesus was God's son. Yet Paul wrote to the church in Rome that "God's eternal power and divine nature have been clearly seen and understood" and that the people "claimed to be wise [but then] became fools [...] exchanging God's glory for images" (Rom 1v18-23). So Paul is not excusing the rulers of this age; more likely, he is saying that God's overall salvation goal was hidden. The means (Christ's death and resurrection) and their achievements were kept a mystery, and therefore could not be thwarted by God's enemies or people's foolishness. These rulers would not and could not have conceived such an unusual yet glorious plan of salvation. And if they could not anticipate it, they could not work against it. In the wisdom and sovereignty of God, their attempt to extinguish Jesus' message by crucifying him became the defining moment of the plan of God's salvation. Amazing.

2:9

> *"However, as it is written:'What no eye has seen, what no ear has heard, and what no human mind has conceived'— the things God has prepared for those who love him—"*

This verse echoes the great prayer of Isaiah 64. It asks for God to rend the heavens, to come down and do awesome things that were not expected. It is a call for God to break in, for Him to unfold His wise plan of salvation. This plan was declared in the Old Testament but the details were scant. A Messiah was promised, but the actual nature and breadth of His mission was inconceivable (Gen 3v15). God had anticipated our rebellion, and has prepared a way to gloriously bring men and women back to Himself (v7). Nothing like this could have been foreseen, heard of or conceived. Illusions and foreshadowings were scattered throughout the Old Testament, but although God's wisdom could be read, it needed to be done in the light of the life, death and resurrection of Jesus.

> *"Although God's wisdom could be read, it needed to be done in the light of the life, death and resurrection of Jesus."*

2:10

"these are the things God has revealed to us by his Spirit. The Spirit searches all things, even the deep things of God."

The mystery that was hidden by God is being revealed by the Spirit of God. What God has hidden will stay hidden until He decides to reveal it. Men and women can not calculate it, discover it, or work it out by themselves. This mystery was hidden in Scripture by the Spirit; now, the same Spirit illuminates the Scripture. The Holy Spirit - the eternal, divine, third person of the Godhead - searches out the deep things of God with the aim of bringing greater glory to the Father and Son. The Spirit brings illumination, wisdom and revelation so that we may know the Father better (Eph 1v17). The Spirit, who proceeds from the Father, is the reliable witness about Jesus (John 15v26). The Spirit, who enjoys eternal and intimate communion with Father and Son, joyfully reveals them to those whom God has called.

> ## "Creatures cannot begin to plumb the thoughts of their Creator"

2:11

"For who knows a person's thoughts except their own spirit within them? In the same way no one knows the thoughts of God except the Spirit of God."

Men and women are well practiced at putting on a game face, and not declaring our true motives or thoughts. Others often don't know what is going on in our hearts and minds. And all of us also know times when we are either unaware of, don't understand, or simply can't articulate what is happening inside of ourselves. Only someone's spirit knows what is going on. If we can't consistently understand and explain ourselves, it is little wonder that we cannot fathom God's thoughts. Creatures cannot begin to plumb the thoughts of their Creator. And yet the one who knows the thoughts of God, the Holy Spirit, graciously reveals the hidden wisdom of salvation to us. The Spirit is the counsellor and the comforter; He who searches out the thoughts of God also comes alongside us and dwells within us.

2:12

"What we have received is not the spirit of the world, but the Spirit who is from God, so that we may understand what God has freely given us."

Paul reminds the Corinthians of a profound benefit of following Christ: that believers receive the Spirit, who is from God. God the Father gives His followers the one who searches out even the deep things of God. The Spirit is not earned, nor is He a reward, but He is given freely to all who believe. The Spirit helps us to understand and grasp the immeasurable riches that are in Christ Jesus. Once again, God gives of Himself: first His Son, now His Spirit. The Spirit's mission is not just to facilitate lively worship (14v26), but also to ensure that we might understand the riches of being in Christ. For example, the Corinthians do not lack any spiritual gift as they eagerly wait for Christ to be revealed (1v7). The wonder and application of that truth needs to be worked into them by the Spirit.

> "Once again, God gives of Himself: first His Son, now His Spirit."

2:13

"This is what we speak, not in words taught us by human wisdom but in words taught by the Spirit, explaining spiritual realities with Spirit-taught words."

Paul confidently asserts his calling as an Apostle of Christ Jesus. The words he spoke were not primarily from his tutor Gamaliel, who trained him according to the strict manner of the Law (Acts 5v34, 22v3). Rather, his words were from Jesus, and were taught by the Holy Spirit. It was the Spirit who illuminated the Old Testament to Paul. It was the Spirit who revealed to him what "no eye has seen, ear has heard, no mind has conceived" (2v10). It was the Spirit who taught him how to express spiritual truth in spiritual words. And these words were confirmed in them (1v6). Paul knew - and even presumed upon - the Spirit's equipping for every season and task he faced. Paul had all he needed, since the Spirit taught him, gifted him and powerfully used him. He who searches the deep truths of God also teaches God's people to express the Gospel truth in powerful ways.

2:14

"The person without the Spirit does not accept the things that come from the Spirit of God but considers them foolishness, and cannot understand them because they are discerned only through the Spirit."

Anyone without the Holy Spirit can no more accept God's wisdom than they can drink salty water. They will simply gag and quickly spit it out, leaving only a bad taste and a raging thirst. The ways of God are foolish and incomprehensible to the unbeliever. The unspiritual person has no capacity to understand the message of the cross nor the things of God. For them it is pure folly, for their minds are in deep darkness and are dull to God's word that brings light. Without the Spirit, only weakness, defeat and shame are visible at Golgotha. Without the Holy Spirit people cannot and will not see; they cannot begin to hear or conceive what God has prepared for them.

2:15

"The person with the Spirit makes judgements about all things, but such a person is not subject to merely human judgements,"

The wisdom given by the Spirit is not without effect. He equips believers to make judgements about relationships, parenting, hospitality, employment, investments, and ethics - to name but a few. The Spirit equips believers to make wise judgements for holy living. Wonderfully, whilst spiritual men and women make judgements, they themselves are not subject to anybody else's judgement. Their judge is Christ alone (2 Tim 4v1). Paul reminds the Colossians not to let anyone "pass judgement on you in questions of food and drink, or with regard to a festival or a new moon or a Sabbath" (Col 2v16). The Spirit teaches them that none of these activities are needed for spiritual advancement or acceptance by the Father. The Spirit equips us to make judgements about our own living, but we are answerable to only one person: Jesus. This verse is rich in gospel freedom and confidence.

> *"Anyone without the Holy Spirit can no more accept God's wisdom than they can drink salty water."*

2:16

"For, 'Who has known the mind of the Lord so as to instruct him?' But we have the mind of Christ."

We read a similar sentiment in Isaiah: "Who has measured the waters in the hollow of his hand or with the breadth of his hand marked off the heavens?" (Isa 40v12). The answer implied here is "no-one". The unbelieving wise man or woman may know many things, but they can never know the mind of Christ. Yet these Corinthians - not many of whom could be considered wise (1v26) - have been given access to and understanding of the mind of Christ by His Spirit (Phil 1v19). Uninfluential people have been welcomed into the treasury of the King's mind. This does not mean that they are equal in knowledge, capacity or experience to Christ. Rather, it means that through the Spirit, their minds are caught up in His desires, wisdom and purposes. Again, Gospel treasure litters these verses. We have all been enriched in every way - even knowing the mind of Christ!

> *"Through the Spirit their minds are caught up in Christ's desires, wisdom and purposes."*

CHAPTER 3

3:1 | *"Brothers and sisters, I could not address you as people who live by the Spirit but as people who are still worldly—mere infants in Christ."*

Paul returns to the glaring issue: the divisions in the Corinthian church. Yes, they are beloved brothers and sisters adopted into God's household. Yes, they have been given much, enriched in every way, and are not lacking any spiritual gift (1v5,7). But their response to this grace is woefully inadequate. They are still living as 'worldly' people; they are living as if they are unaware (or have forgotten) that Christ has become their wisdom, righteousness, holiness and redemption. They argue and divide over which of Jesus' apostles they prefer to follow. Paul contrasts this 'worldly' behaviour against being 'spiritual' - that is, being perfectly united in mind and thought (1v10). The Corinthians are acting as though they have an unredeemed human nature, with all its desires and behaviours.

> *"Their response to this grace is woefully inadequate."*

3:2 | *"I gave you milk, not solid food, for you were not yet ready for it. Indeed, you are still not ready."*

Paul has circled back to Chloe's household concerns, quarrels among the Corinthian church over apostles. In Paul's mind, jealousy and division and arguments have nothing to do with God, who is love and community. They are still worldly rather than Godly, and so he is reluctant to teach them more until they have grasped the infant teaching of unity, peace and love. They were acting like mere men, of which they are so much more! Factions, envy and division should have no place amongst God's household who have the Spirit of God among them. Paul reprimands them but calls them still worldly because of their jealousy and quarrelling among them. Their eyes were off the Christ and on his sent ones...the fruit being division.

3:3

"You are still worldly. For since there is jealousy and quarelling among you, are you not worldly? Are you not acting like mere humans?"

Paul has circled back to the concern expressed by someone from Chloe's household: their quarelling over apostles. To Paul's mind, jealousy, division and arguments were hallmarks of worldliness. The church was acting like unregenerate people who had never heard the good news of Jesus. These traits have nothing in common with God, who is a community of love. Factions and envy should be unthinkable amongst those in whom the Spirit of God dwells. Paul reprimands the Corinthians, telling them they are still "worldly" despite the extended time he spent with them, and the teaching of Cephas and Apollos. Their eyes had lost focus on Christ and were fixed on the people He sent.

"He and Apollos are not alternative figureheads of a new humanity, nor the Deans of alternative schools of philosophy."

3:4

"For when one says, 'I follow Paul,' and another, 'I follow Apollos,' are you not mere human beings?"

Presumably Paul is quoting the verbal report of conversations in Corinth, here. He is dismissive of their reported thinking. He and Apollos are not alternative figureheads of a new humanity, nor the Deans of alternative schools of philosophy. They are merely servants of a much greater teacher. For the Corinthians even to think this way demonstrates their spiritual immaturity. They are still speaking from the script of a fallen humanity rather than from the story of heaven. "Mere human beings" attempt to "build a city with a tower that reaches to the heavens in order to make a name for themselves" (Gen 11v4). "Mere human beings" want to be ruled by their own monarchs, and to worship gods of their own making. But in Jesus' kingdom, He is the undisputed King. He is the principal character, the great Teacher, the Victor, the Champion, the Prophet, the Priest, and the King. To focus on following a servant when you have been given access to the great King makes no sense.

3:5 | *"What, after all, is Apollos? And what is Paul? Only servants, through whom you came to believe—as the Lord has assigned to each his task."*

The Corinthians were arguing about who to follow, so Paul reminds them that apostles are merely servants of Christ Jesus (see also Phil 1v1, Titus 1v1). Paul and Apollos, along with Cephas and others, are merely 'sent ones' with appointed tasks: Apollos and Paul were to herald the gospel and reap salvation on behalf of Christ their master. Each has a unique role to play, and has received grace and gifting accordingly. It was the Lord who called Paul and assigned him his task - not on the basis of any previous good works, but solely because of grace and God's wisdom. Paul is delighted that his testimony about Christ was confirmed in them (1v6), but he was only doing what he was called to do. He proclaims Christ. He builds people to Christ. The servants do their Master's bidding: it is for His glory, not theirs.

3:6 | *"I planted the seed, Apollos watered it, but God has been making it grow."*

Paul uses a farming metaphor to help the Corinthians see their condition; these infants in Christ need simple pictures. Creation speaks clearly to us, and no image is more familiar than the basic pattern of planting and watering a seed, before watching a plant grow. Yes, someone has to plant and water the seed, but the real wonder comes in the growth. The simple activities of planting and watering are quickly eclipsed by the mystery of life emerging from inert matter. Pushing something into dirt or pouring water are simple and relatively unskilled processes. Creating a suitable environment to help something grow can be challenging, but making it grow is beyond us. Here, then, is a lesson from farming that elevates Christ and unites the church. Apollos - a learned man with a thorough knowledge of Scripture, who spoke with fervour and accuracy about Jesus - merely waters the gospel seed that had been planted by another (Acts 18v24-25). All glory should go to the one who made it grow.

> *"Here, then, is a lesson from farming that elevates Christ and unites the church."*

3:7

"So neither the one who plants nor the one who waters is anything, but only God, who makes things grow."

In contrast with the miracle of making something grow, planting and watering are trivial activities that require little talent or skill. So while Paul affirms that he is an apostle (1v1), bearing a message of wisdom (2v6), and has the mind of Christ (2v16b), he is clear that in comparison to God's part in saving people he is of little standing. Jesus is the big story and the prime mover. Jesus makes things grow. We know that "a man scatters seed on the ground, night and day, whether he sleeps or gets up, the seed sprouts and grows; and he knows not how" (Mark 4v26-27). But the gospel seed that was scattered by a Jew from Tarsus and watered by a Jew from Alexandria (Acts 18v24) is given life by Jesus. Only God can make the gospel seed take root in people's hearts, and only God can grow it. He does that for His glory, and He will not share that with anyone except His Son and His Spirit.

3:8

"The one who plants and the one who waters have one purpose, and they will each be rewarded according to their own labour."

The purpose of a good servant is to please their master, and they should be content with their master's reward. If the master is wise and faithful, he will reward according to each servant's work and endeavour. God is a good master: "God is not unjust; He will not forget your work and the love you have shown Him as you have helped His people and continue to help them" (Heb 6v10). Both Paul and Apollos have laboured for God, sowing and watering. Their reward is from heaven, and not from men. They look to their heavenly master - not to his household - for their approval and recompense. Single-minded men and women can achieve much, especially when they join forces to go about the business of their collective master. And each will be rewarded: God is not unjust.

"They look to their heavenly master - not to his household - for their approval and recompense"

3:9 | *"For we are co-workers in God's service; you are God's field, God's building."*

The metaphor changes here, from agriculture to construction. Paul and Apollos are fellow workers for God; they are joined by a common cause and endeavour. They are like farmers and builders; they are both colleagues and partners. No single metaphor can depict the richness and glory of how God fathers, shepherds, cultivates and builds His people. The Corinthians would have been familiar with both fields and temples, and with the way in which farmers and builders worked together to produce something. Paul and Apollos are not in competition, nor are they working on alternative projects; they are fellow workers in God's field, and fellow workers on God's building. Apollos and Paul both labour amongst God's people, albeit in the different seasons of farm life or in the different stages in the construction of a building. Paul is writing to restore unity in the Corinthian church by helping them to better understand how apostles work amongst them.

> *"Grace gives Paul confidence to assert the task and gifting he has been given"*

3:10 | *"By the grace God has given me, I laid a foundation as a wise builder, and someone else is building on it. But each one should build with care."*

Paul presumably includes a reference to God's grace to underline that his calling is not on his own merits. Grace gives Paul confidence to assert the task and gifting he has been given: he is a skilled master builder, who has laid an excellent foundation. Grace allows us to 'boast' in Christ Jesus. The one who once tried to tear down God's house, who was heard "breathing out murderous threats against the Lord's disciples, who sought permission to go to the synagogue in Damascus to arrest anyone following the way" (Acts 9v1-2), has been given the grace to become an expert builder of God's: the very thing he once tried to destroy! The man who went to Damascus to tear down went to Corinth to lay the perfect foundation. Grace builds for God; grace releases what is God's. Paul is happy for others to build on his foundation: it is God's building, not his.

3:11

> *"For no one can lay any foundation other than the one already laid, which is Jesus Christ."*

Many apostles and teachers had passed through Corinth - its geography made it that kind of place. Unfortunately, the believers' preferences became prejudices, and divisions arose amongst them. Paul argues that the apostles all are fellow construction workers, working on the same foundation: Jesus. When he states that "no-one can lay any [other] foundation", he is not saying that it would be impossible to do so. Indeed, the Galatians started with Christ but then turned to a different gospel, leaving Paul astonished (Gal 1v6-7). Rather, he is declaring Christ to be the only foundation worth building upon: everything else will give way and collapse, much like building on sand. In Corinth's melting pot of Roman, Greek and Jewish cultures, along with many others, there were many pressures to cut corners on the 'groundwork' that was hidden out of sight. The message of Christ must be fully preached into every context, He is the foundation that must be received and built upon.

"Unfortunately, the believers' preferences became prejudices, and divisions arose amongst them."

3:12-13a

> *"If anyone builds on this foundation using gold, silver, costly stones, wood, hay or straw, their work will be shown for what it is, because the Day will bring it to light."*

Given Paul's extended building metaphor, it is not unreasonable here to see a parallel with the construction of Solomon's temple. That Old Testament king also used gold, silver, precious stones, bronze and wood (1 Chro 3v12) for the construction of "the house of my God". Solomon's temple was built at a great cost to God's people; hopefully their hearts inclined to where they invested their treasure. And the glory and wonder of the resplendent building spoke for itself. How each apostle builds on the foundation of Christ will be tested; it will make itself known on the judgement day. All will be tested, apostles and saints; they are all building on the same foundation. Some build at great personal cost and with devotion; others build using cheaper materials. But everyone's work will be shown for what it is, because "the Day" will bring it to light. This term refers to the day of judgement, when all will stand before the judgment seat of Christ (Rev 20v12).

3:13 | *"It will be revealed with fire, and the fire will test the quality of each person's work."*

In his letter to the church in Rome, Paul states: "For we will all stand before the judgement seat of God [...] each of us will give an account of himself to God" (Rom 14v10). And the church in Galatia were warned: "Do not be deceived: God is not mocked, for whatever one sows, that will he also reap" (Gal 6v7). Whatever we build with will be tested; the quality of our work and the materials used will be subjected to judgement. Just as gold is refined and tested by fire, so will Christians' work be subjected to the righteous gaze of God. He who gave His Son as the foundation to be built upon will also determine the quality of the builders' labour. The Corinthians' salvation was already assured - it is by grace, through faith (Eph 2v8) - but they may not be accruing eternal rewards. This is both a warning to those tempted to cut corners, and an encouragement to those who faithfully build at great cost to themselves. God is not fooled. His furnace, his crucible, will give a true assessment of the quality of our labour in Christ.

3:14 | *"If what has been built survives, the builder will receive a reward."*

All of the apostles will have their work tested. God's "fire" - His judgement - will assess the quality of their work. Their right standing before God is not being called into question; like all believers they have been justified by faith: "Therefore, since we have been justified by faith, we have peace with God through our Lord Jesus Christ" (Rom 5v1). They will not face condemnation: "There is therefore now no condemnation for those who are in Christ Jesus" (Rom 8v1). But God will still judge their work and reward them accordingly: "we will all stand before the judgement seat of God" (Rom 14v10). God will reward the good that is done in his name, even if no-one else knows about it (Matt 6v1-6). Apostles can only profitably build on the foundation of Christ; it matters little who had the best preaching style or the biggest following in Corinth. These worldly successes are of little substance compared with obedience and faithfulness when proclaiming the message of Christ.

> *"This is both a warning to those tempted to cut corners, and an encouragement to those who faithfully build at great cost"*

3:15

> *"If it is burned up, the builder will suffer loss but yet will be saved—even though only as one escaping through the flames."*

Apostles will be saved, that much is assured, but they will also be tested. The hope is that much of what they have built will endure, and that they are rewarded accordingly. But it does seem possible that what an apostle has built could be mostly burnt up, and as a result he could gain little - if any - accrued reward. These are encouraging yet sobering verses. But they don't only apply to apostles or church leaders; they apply to anyone who contributes in any way to building up the church. Later in the letter, Paul writes "To each is given the manifestation of the Spirit for the common good" (1 Cor 12v7). He will go on to say that the church is a body of many members, and that all the members are equipped and required to help build up the one body. Each of us plays our part in strengthening the church; how we do this, and what we contribute, will be tested. God willing, we will be rewarded. Our salvation is assured; our reward is yet to be reckoned.

> ## *"Our salvation is assured; our reward is yet to be reckoned."*

3:16

> *"Don't you know that you yourselves are God's temple and that God's Spirit dwells in your midst?"*

A temple is a place dedicated to the worship of a deity. God's people had built three successively in Jerusalem: Solomon's, Zerubbabel's, and Herod's. Yet the temple that Paul refers to now is not a place but a people. Once God dwelt above the mercy seat in the Tabernacle in the desert (Exo 25v8), and then in the stone Temple in Jerusalem (2 Chron 7v1). But now God's presence is within his people by His Spirit. They are made holy by faith in Christ, and become the dwelling place of God by His Spirit; they are the new Temple of living stones (1 Peter 2v5). The Place has become a People; a Building has become Flesh. God no longer dwells amongst us as He did in Moses' time, or even as in the time before Jesus' resurrection. Now God dwells within us by His Spirit! As such, there can be no place for division in God's Temple; His glory should eclipse the jealousy and quarrelling (3v3) in the church.

3:17

"If anyone destroys God's temple, God will destroy that person; for God's temple is sacred, and you together are that temple."

Paul was a Jew who knew his history, and that included the destruction of Solomon's temple by the Babylonians and Zerubbabel's temple by the Romans. These acts of desecration by God's enemies brought retribution to the perpetrators. Just as these physical temples were destroyed, so too can the living stones of the church be pulled apart by disunity and forgetting the foundation of Christ. The perpetrators of this desecration of the temple of living stones would also be punished.

To summarise, Paul's train of thought seems to be that true apostles build on the foundation of Christ, and even if they build with straw - which will be burned up - they will be saved. Apostles who don't build on Christ destroy God's temple, and will therefore be destroyed themselves.

3:18

"Do not deceive yourselves. If any of you think you are wise by the standards of this age, you should become 'fools' so that you may become wise."

Paul started Chapter 3 with a rebuke: that the Corinthians were still mere infants in Christ, not yet ready for solid food. No doubt this was offensive - and for a reason. Presumably some of the Corinthian believers were educated, enjoyed good social standing, and had a measure of social wisdom - although Paul does admit that "not many of you were wise by human standard nor influential" (1v26). They - like us - were prone to deceive themselves, thinking that they knew a lot more than they actually did. Just because they have figured out how to do 'life' well, that does not automatically translate into knowing how to do 'spiritual life' well. The antidote to deceiving themselves in this manner is to let the foolishness of the cross seep into their hearts (1v18,20). Paul encourages them to become foolish so that they may become truly wise – the wisdom of this age is too small a prize when God's wisdom is on offer.

> *"The wisdom of this age is too small a prize when God's wisdom is on offer"*

3:19

> *"For the wisdom of this world is foolishness in God's sight. As it is written:'He catches the wise in their craftiness;'"*

People can never, nor have ever, outwitted God. For all our wisdom and achievements, for all our understanding and accomplishments, we are still finite, created beings; we are creatures whose existence is sustained by the Creator. Our greatest moments are just moments in which we think we are great. They pale into insignificance when compared to the eternal and infinite wisdom of the all-knowing Creator. We can never fool, deceive, outshine or eclipse God's wisdom. He can see through all our schemes. He easily catches us in our crafty and cunning plans. We still endeavour to get the upper hand, as if that were at all possible; finite wisdom appeals because we can only grasp the finite. The wisdom of this world is exalted by those clamouring for attention, wisdom and success. Yet God opposes the proud; their wily schemes are swept away like the dust clinging to a trophy case.

3:20

> *"and again, 'The Lord knows that the thoughts of the wise are futile.'"*

Paul started this section by calling the Corinthians "worldly" and spiritual babies (3v1), and warning them against considering themselves to be wise. To drive this point further he quotes from Psalm 94v11. Here, the writer is calling God to rise up and pay back the proud and the wicked, who pour out arrogant words and merciless actions against God's people. They are deluded by their own wisdom; they are senseless ones, fools who think God is blind and deaf. The very ones who say "The Lord does not see, the God of Jacob pays no heed" (Psalm 94v7) are known by the Lord. God sees their raging ways and thoughts and considers them futile; these fools will be paid back for what they deserve. Here, Paul is hammering his point home to the Corinthian believers: God will judge and destroy anyone who pulls apart His precious temple - His people, His church.

> *"Our greatest moments are just moments in which we think we are great."*

3:21-22

"So then, no more boasting about human leaders! All things are yours, whether Paul or Apollos or Cephas or the world or life or death or the present or the future— all are yours,"

The Corinthians had settled for identifying with a mere apostle. And so they argued, divided and boasted accordingly, to elevate their choice. Few of the Corinthians were wise, influential or of noble birth when they were saved (1v26), yet now they quarrelled as if they had great knowledge. But it was Christ who enriched them in every way (1v4). It was Christ who became their wisdom, righteousness, holiness and redemption (1v30). It was because of Christ that all things were now theirs. They were once foolish and lowly, but now they are caught up with all those everywhere who call on the name of the Lord. They are now grafted into an ancient vine, a greater story - along with Paul, Apollos, Peter, the world, life, death, the present and the future. Everything now would be worked and wrapped together for their good. And this was because of Christ, not Paul, Apollos or Cephas! They were now in Christ - not in a mere apostle.

"If they are in Christ, and all things are theirs, what else is there to desire?"

3:23

"and you are of Christ, and Christ is of God."

Galatians 3v29 records "if you are Christ's, then you are Abraham's offspring, heirs according to the promise". Abraham's offspring were blessed and were to be a blessing to the nations of the world. If anyone was part of the family of Abraham then they were included in that ancient promise. In the same way, the Corinthians are now included in Christ and will receive his promise of life to the full. They are in Christ, and Christ is in God. And if they are now in God, why should they boast about who baptised them?! If they are in Christ, and all things are theirs, what else is there to desire? This is why Paul cannot address the Corinthians as spiritually wise or mature (3v1): because they cannot see the full riches they have in Christ. Paul urges that there should be "no more boasting about men!". Because of Christ alone, the Corinthians now have all things. They are of Christ, who created, sustains and rules over all. They are of Christ, and Christ is of God.

CHAPTER 4

4:1 | *"This, then, is how you ought to regard us: as servants of Christ and as those entrusted with the mysteries God has revealed."*

Paul had urged the Corinthians to stop boasting about apostles; instead, they were to regard them as those entrusted with the secret things of God. The Corinthians needed to hold the tension of esteeming but not elevating. By the grace of God, Paul was an expert builder (3v10) on the foundation of Christ - yet he did not preach to them with wise and eloquent words. He came to them in fear and trembling (2v3), whilst knowing he was entrusted with God's secret wisdom, revealed by the Spirit (2v10). Each servant of God was assigned a task (3v5): Paul planted, Apollos watered. They were mere servants, but they faithfully stewarded the gospel message with a demonstration of the Spirit's power (2v4). When thinking of apostles, Paul encourages the Corinthians to tolerate the tension of giving honour whilst receiving them as servants.

> *"It is difficult to imagine anything more valuable than the Gospel of Salvation."*

4:2 | *"Now it is required that those who have been given a trust must prove faithful."*

Apostles are stewards of the mysteries of God. The ESV puts the verse this way: "it is required of stewards that they be found trustworthy". Paul, Apollos and Cephas had the Gospel of Jesus Christ revealed to them by God through his Spirit (2v10). This came with significant responsibility: it required them to be found trustworthy and proven faithful. In Luke 12, Jesus told a parable of two stewards: one who behaved well in his master's absence, and one who did not. Jesus concluded this teaching by saying "Everyone to whom much was given, of him much will be required, and from him to whom they entrusted much, they will demand the more" (Luke 12v48). It is difficult to imagine anything more valuable than the Gospel of Salvation. If apostles are given the high privilege of stewarding such riches, then they must be proven faithful and trustworthy.

4:3

> *"I care very little if I am judged by you or by any human court; indeed, I do not even judge myself."*

Paul considers himself to be a steward who must be proved faithful and trustworthy. This implies that he will be assessed on how well he has fulfilled his duties as an apostle of Christ. While he is on earth, this assessment will be done by many parties, but for Paul, the only judgement that counts is God's. As Paul stewards the mysteries of God, he cares little for the score cards given by the beneficiaries of his service. Paul's ear is turned instead to his Heavenly Master's opinion. The context for these remarkable statements is the playing off of one servant against another: is Cephas or Apollos or Paul the better steward? Paul has no time for this childish and immature approach; his gaze and the source of his affirmation transcends their transitory approval. It is worth noting that he doesn't even judge himself. These are wise words, given that our feelings, circumstances and measures of success can be as changing as the seasons.

> *"These are wise words, given that our feelings, circumstances and measures of success can be as changing as the seasons."*

4:4

> *"My conscience is clear, but that does not make me innocent. It is the Lord who judges me."*

Some of the Corinthians were speaking negatively about Paul, presumably because he did not come to them preaching with wisdom or eloquence (1v17, 2v1). Some thought they were able and qualified to judge his spiritual effectiveness - and they found him lacking. Yet Paul is not aware of any such shortcomings; when he searches his own soul against such criticism it reveals nothing. Nevertheless, he entrusts the final assessment of his innocence to Christ. To the Christian, our God-given moral compass, our conscience, is both a gift to be used and a plant to be nurtured. Our conscience is corrupted and hardened by sin and needs to be nurtured to life and health by the Spirit, who illuminates God's Word. Our conscience judges us, but it cannot make us innocent or acquit us of sin. Instead, our conscience points to the courtroom of God. It is the Lord who will judge us all. And it is the Lord who will assess Paul's ministry. Corinthian opinion matters little.

4:5

> "*Therefore judge nothing before the appointed time; wait until the Lord comes. He will bring to light what is hidden in darkness and will expose the motives of the heart. At that time each will receive their praise from God.*"

Paul is certain that a day of reckoning is coming, and he has this in mind when considering public opinion or facing criticism. He reminds his readers that they, too, will have the motives of their hearts searched and judged. Whatever is hidden in darkness will be brought into the light. The phrase "hidden in darkness" speaks of secret sin; perhaps Paul has in mind those who have become arrogant and spoken out against him (4v18). Paul consoles himself by waiting for vindication from the Lord. All servants do well when they have their master's approval at the front and centre in their thinking and motives. The servant with a just and wise master has nothing to fear, as long as they are a faithful steward. How much more can Paul be confident of a fair and wise assessment of his service from God? This most just master will be sure to give appropriate praise.

4:6

> "*Now, brothers and sisters, I have applied these things to myself and Apollos for your benefit, so that you may learn from us the meaning of the saying, 'Do not go beyond what is written.' Then you will not be puffed up in being a follower of one of us over against the other.*"

So far in his letter, Paul has made five references to the Old Testament: he quotes Isaiah 29v14, "I will destroy the wisdom of the wise, the intelligence of the intelligent I will frustrate" (1v19); Jeremiah 9v22-23, "Let him who boasts, boast in the Lord" (1v31); Isaiah 64v4, "No eye has seen, no ear has heard, no mind has conceived what God has prepared for those who love him" (2v9); Job 5v13, "He catches the wise in their craftiness" (3v19); and Psalm 94v11, "The Lord knows that the thoughts of the wise are futile" (3v20). Paul wants Scripture to shape the Corinthians' thinking and attitudes. Had they allowed the scripture to do so, they would have avoided many of their divisions and arguments.

> "*Paul consoles himself by waiting for vindication from the Lord.*"

4:7

> *"For who makes you different from anyone else? What do you have that you did not receive? And if you did receive it, why do you boast as though you did not?"*

Here, then, is the nub of the truth that Paul is highlighting: in all their divisions the Corinthians have lost sight of grace. Everything that they have was not a result of their own efforts or received on their own merit but given as a grace gift from God. They boast because they have forgotten - or neglected to cultivate - this central truth. Had they kept God's grace in their minds and conversations, no doubt it would have produced unity, humility and thanksgiving. All their opportunities, gifts and blessings are gifts from a generous God. He has no favourites, so they should not boast. It is thanks to God the Father that they are in Christ Jesus, so "Let the one who boasts, boast in the Lord" (1v30).

4:8

> *"Already you have all you want! Already you have become rich! You have begun to reign—and that without us! How I wish that you really had begun to reign so that we also might reign with you!"*

Paul uses irony and humour here to bring home his point. Not many of the Corinthians were wise, influential or noble, yet now they boast like kings. They have become haughty, like a well-established king who reigns with great riches. The result of their woefully deficient understanding of grace is a transformation in their opinion of themselves from 'nobodies' to 'mighty kings'. Paul teases them by playing along, wishing he could join them in reigning in their 'mighty kingship'. They consider themselves special, wise and worthy because they have forgotten that they received everything as a gift. These Corinthian 'kings' are quick to herald their assessments and opinions, yet their only real reason for boasting is Christ (1v31).

> *"Had they kept God's grace in their minds and conversations, no doubt it would have produced unity, humility and thanksgiving."*

4:9

> *"For it seems to me that God has put us apostles
> on display at the end of the procession, like those
> condemned to die in the arena. We have been made
> a spectacle to the whole universe, to angels as well
> as to human beings."*

Paul is referring here to the Roman victory parade. Tradition existed that after a successful military battle, the victorious Roman army would process back into their home city. At the very end of this parade were the conquered and captured soldiers and civilians. They would be led through streets full of jeering citizens before being publicly executed. The purpose of this procession was simple: to make it clear who was victorious and knew glory and who was defeated and knew shame. So while the Corinthians boast and jockey for status, Paul pictures the apostles as captured men condemned to die. The contrast could not be starker: the 'kings of Corinth' are compared with the 'condemned apostles'. Paul sees his life as a spectacle to the whole universe. The servants of Christ are last, are shunned and shamed by the world, and this is purposed by God. There can be no room for spiritual elitism or pride amongst those who have yielded their life to Christ.

*"While the Corinthians boast and jockey for status,
Paul pictures the apostles as captured men
condemned to die."*

4:10

> *"We are fools for Christ, but you are so wise in
> Christ! We are weak, but you are strong! You are
> honored, we are dishonored!"*

Paul continues his playful contrasts, but his point is barbed. Despite their apparent zeal for following in the footsteps of their favourite apostle, the Corinthians are out of step with apostolic thinking. God has made the apostles a spectacle of foolishness, weakness and dishonour. Apostles are much like the people at the wrong end of the victory procession: they are defeated soldiers given over to public scorn, shame, and a humiliating death. Yet the Corinthians argue over which apostle to follow, seemingly unaware of their imminent public death. They regard themselves as wise, strong and honoured, yet they also claim to follow those who are being shamed. This makes no sense. Few cultures honour and esteem the qualities of foolishness, weakness and dishonour, and yet God will choose these virtues to fulfil his purposes. When these are present, it's as though God's goodness, wisdom and mercy are easier to see. His glory is magnified when He works through foolish, weak and dishonoured people.

4:11-12

"To this very hour we go hungry and thirsty, we are in rags, we are brutally treated, we are homeless. We work hard with our own hands. When we are cursed, we bless; when we are persecuted, we endure it;"

In contrast with those in Corinth who considered themselves kings, Paul's life was very different. Being a servant of Christ - being entrusted with the secret things of God - involved hardship and suffering. Paul tells the Corinthians of his current situation in Ephesus: he goes hungry and thirsty; he wears rags; he is homeless; and he is brutally treated. This expert church planter, who lays theological foundations that others build upon (3v10), also uses his own hands to provide for himself: we are told in Acts 18v3 that he was a tentmaker. Paul, unlike a king, did not presume upon his subjects to provide for him. Rather, he worked to meet his own needs (1Thess 2v9). When he was criticised, he spoke well of his accusers. When he was persecuted, he endured. As it was with Jesus, so it goes for those who follow Him: no servant is greater than his master (John 15v20). The Corinthians needed a reminder of the apostolic teaching on enduring hardship and suffering for the gospel.

> *"As it was with Jesus, so it goes for those who follow Him."*

4:13

"when we are slandered, we answer kindly. We have become the scum of the earth, the garbage of the world—right up to this moment."

This is not an attractive job description, to be considered a Fool for Christ, to be a spectacle of shame to the whole universe, to be considered the scum of the earth. Paul keeps driving the point home: the Corinthians argue and create factions over which scum to follow, which refuse of the world to align themselves to. Apostles have been entrusted with much and are authenticated by a demonstration of the Spirit's power (2v4). But this role also attracts great hardship and ignominy. When apostles are slandered they answer kindly; they respond only to ensure that the gospel message is not brought into disrepute. This was Paul's ongoing experience; he had been unwanted, discarded, and reviled by the world "up to this moment". Apostles endured physical hardship and public scorn - it came with the job. These are strong words. Those who are entrusted with the "secret things of God" (4v1) are not superstars but servants - they serve the One who was also regarded by the world as scum and refuse.

4:14-15

"I am writing this not to shame you but to warn you as my dear children. Even if you had ten thousand guardians in Christ, you do not have many fathers, for in Christ Jesus I became your father through the gospel."

Just as a father warns his child of danger, so Paul warns the Corinthians about their trajectory. Pride, division, and quarrelling over which apostle to follow are of grave concern. While Paul acknowledges the helpful contribution that others have made to the church's development (3v6, 16v12), he has a unique 'fathering' relationship with them. He first went to Corinth and reasoned in their synagogue, and then in the house of Titus Justus. Their church was established through his preaching. Fathers are to bring life, identity, discipline, and direction. He admonishes them just as a father does for his children. His love for them propels him to guide them. His motive is not to shame, but to bring life and health. The relationship between an apostle and a church is described here in warm, familial language. This is not the language of allocated supervision within an impersonal organisation.

4:16

"Therefore I urge you to imitate me."

Paul unashamedly urges the Corinthians to imitate him - he is at the back of the procession, enduring hardship, and thought of as scum. But they have been far from doing that. While they jockey for position, Paul considers himself a servant. While they act like kings, Paul is led into the arena to be killed. He wants them to grasp that progress in the Christian life can be made by imitating others in the ways they follow Christ. Simply following another's example can be a 'concrete' next step in discipleship. Paul urged the Philippians similarly: "Brothers, join in imitating me, and keep your eyes on those who walk according to the example you have in us" (Phil 3v17). To the Thessalonians, he said "For you yourselves know how you ought to imitate us" (2 Thess 3v7). To Titus he wrote "show yourself in all respects to be a model of good works" (Titus 2v7).

> *"Fathers are to bring life, identity, discipline, and direction."*

4:17

> "For this reason I have sent to you Timothy, my son whom I love, who is faithful in the Lord. He will remind you of my way of life in Christ Jesus, which agrees with what I teach everywhere in every church."

When Paul went to Lystra he met a disciple named Timothy, whose mother was a believing Jew and whose father was a Greek. Paul decided to take Timothy with him on his apostolic journey, and so began a fruitful apostolic relationship (Acts 16v1-5). Timothy was more than a team member: Paul loved him as a son, and Timothy took on Paul's way of life in Christ Jesus. He was a delegate of Paul's ministry, he embodied Paul's message and passion. Timothy was not a clone of Paul, but he has taken on the family likeness to such an extent that Paul considers him a true spiritual son. He was well able to remind the various factions about Paul's original teachings. Paul also reminds the Corinthians that not only does he father Timothy and their church, but also other churches in other places. They are part of a much bigger family, and are not free to go alone!

> *"Holiness, unity and peace were hard won at the cross, and the Spirit still works jealously for them."*

4:18-19

> "Some of you have become arrogant, as if I were not coming to you. But I will come to you very soon, if the Lord is willing, and then I will find out not only how these arrogant people are talking, but what power they have."

Some of the Corinthians had an exaggerated sense of their own importance and abilities. Talk is cheap, and a few in the church thought he wasn't returning to call them to account. They had become puffed up and detached from their founding father who, God willing, was intending to visit. Paul, the servant of Christ, was planning on wielding some of his Master's power. He expects a confrontation - perhaps like that with Ananias and Sapphira, who tried to deceive the apostles and test the Spirit of God (Acts 5v1-11). Certainly, Paul expects for the Spirit to vindicate him. Holiness, unity and peace were hard won at the cross, and the Spirit still works jealously for them. All churches need a father to call them out on their blind spots, and for the Spirit to demonstrate His power.

4:20

> *"For the kingdom of God is not a matter of talk but of power."*

Taken in isolation, this verse can easily be misunderstood. Paul is not boasting of an apostolic 'power play', where the greatest supernatural demonstration wins. Rather, he is saying that his true apostleship will be accompanied by supernatural endorsement. A demonstration of the Spirit's power will authenticate his fathering of the Corinthians, over and above the arrogant talkers in the church. His message was not delivered "with wise and persuasive words, but with a demonstration of the Spirit's power, so that their faith might not rest on men's wisdom, but on God's power" (2v4-5). The Spirit will testify to the servant of Christ through works of supernatural power. Paul is living with an expectation of power demonstrations to attest to his apostleship will be attested to by demonstrations of power.

4:21

> *"What do you prefer? Shall I come to you with a rod of discipline, or shall I come in love and with a gentle spirit?"*

Context is everything! Taken in isolation, this would be a very curious verse. But it makes sense as the continuation of Paul's comments above: the loving words of a spiritual father bringing correction to wayward individuals within a church. This rhetorical question has only one expected answer: they would want him to visit with a gentle and loving spirit. His desire is for all of the Corinthians to continue in a good relationship with their father in Christ. Yet he must address the divisive teachers and influences within their fellowship. In the same way, God sent His Son to us - not with a whip to beat us into submission, but with a gentle and loving spirit. Why was it this way? Because He wants to win our hearts, not simply to change our behaviour. Our rebellion and sinfulness do need to be addressed, but not in the way we might have expected. The end was achieved, but the means was surprising. Love trumps the rod.

> *"God sent His Son to us - not with a whip to beat us into submission, but with a gentle and loving spirit."*

CHAPTER 5

5:1 | *"It is actually reported that there is sexual immorality among you, and of a kind that even pagans do not tolerate: A man is sleeping with his father's wife."*

This sexual immorality has been brought to Paul's attention, presumably by those of Chloe's household (1v11). Most likely, it is between a son and his stepmother; Paul would have been explicit if it were the biological mother. Leviticus 18v8 forbids this: "Do not have sexual relations with your father's wife; that would dishonour your father". 'Sexual relations' is a common Old Testament euphemism for sexual intercourse. Ironically, the Corinthian Christians were more tolerant of flagrant sexual sin than the pagans among whom they lived. Grace is profoundly simple, yet easily misunderstood. Grace calls for holiness, not for toleration of sin.

> ## *"Grace is profoundly simple, yet easily misunderstood."*

5:2 | *"And you are proud! Shouldn't you rather have gone into mourning and have put out of your fellowship the man who has been doing this?"*

God's people were supposed to be distinct, to be set apart and to stand out as holy. In the Old Testament this was governed by strict codes of practice and regulations. The Israelites' pursuit of holiness was a significant part of being counted as God's people. This requirement had not changed under the new covenant, yet the Corinthians had lost sight of this. For Paul, it was obvious that they should put the immoral brother under church discipline: how could they tolerate such obvious sinfulness amongst them? Worse, they were proud - perhaps they thought it spoke better of the grace of God (Rom 6v1). The Corinthians had lost sight of the sinfulness of sin and the holiness of God. They should have been mourning, and removed this man from their fellowship. But they were more concerned with their allegiance to apostles (1v12) than with living the holiness won for them by Jesus. **Question:** What sin and rebellion am I tolerating?

5:3

"For my part, even though I am not physically present, I am with you in spirit. As one who is present with you in this way, I have already passed judgment in the name of our Lord Jesus on the one who has been doing this."

Paul is not suggesting that he is so holy he is omnipresent (present everywhere at the same time). This cannot be what he means! Rather, he clearly feels joined in heart to them; he has written of being their father through the gospel (4v15). Paul's strength of affection for the Corinthians causes the distance between them to melt away. His concern and love for them propels him to pass and pronounce judgement on wayward members of the church. Just as a father cheers his child from the seats of the stadium, as if he were right alongside them on the running track, so Paul is caught up in the Corinthian family and their challenges. Paul has heard enough about the Corinthians' activities to make a sound judgement, so they should too.

> *"Paul's strength of affection for the Corinthians causes the distance between them to melt away."*

5:4

"So when you are assembled and I am with you in spirit, and the power of our Lord Jesus is present,"

Here we must make sense of the phrase "with you in spirit". Nowhere else does scripture allude to someone's spirit being present outside of their situation or location. We must arrive at an understanding that lets the rest of scripture interpret and be in harmony with the meaning here. When Jesus says "when two or three are gathered there I am also" (Matt 18v20), it implies that Jesus' rule and influence is there (as well as that Jesus himself is present by His spirit). So Paul is most likely saying that when the church gathers in the name of Jesus, and the power of the Holy Spirit is present, then the influence of His delegate Paul will inevitably be present, as Paul is the founding apostle and spiritual father. Paul's influence and teaching is likely to be particularly manifested in difficult moments, such as when church discipline is being worked out. He is present in the sense that the church is acting upon his instruction and teaching.

5:5 | *"hand this man over to Satan for the destruction of the flesh, so that his spirit may be saved on the day of the Lord."*

Here we see the purpose of church discipline: the immoral brother is put out of fellowship, with the aim that he will be saved on the day of judgement. Satan is a real being; the world is his domain (Eph 2v2), and is in his power (1 John 5v19). The Church is to trust that God is able to redeem the immoral believer, even when he has been handed over for Satan to destroy his sinful nature. Satan may be able to kill the body, but he cannot kill a man's soul; that is God's prerogative (Matt 10v28). The believer is delivered over to Satan, but Satan is not on his side. Satan remains a servant of God, albeit a rebellious one. In the Old Testament, Job was handed over to Satan, even though he was blameless and upright - we read that Job feared God and turned from evil (Job 1v1). Just as Job was vindicated by God, so Paul hopes this wayward believer will be redeemed.

5:6 | *"Your boasting is not good. Don't you know that a little yeast leavens the whole batch of dough?"*

Yeast as we know it, sold dried and in packets, was obviously not available in Paul's day. Rather, they would let dough ferment, so that a fungus consumeed the sugar and excreted carbon dioxide causing the bread to rise. A small amount of fermented dough would then be worked through new dough, with a dramatic effect. Paul likens the Corinthians' boasting to yeast. Their loud, positive self-appraisal was puffing themselves up; outwardly they looked and sounded far more impressive than they were. And this was not in keeping with Paul's spiritual diagnosis of them. While he thanked God for the grace given to them, Paul is concerned that their pride and boasting will work its way through all areas of church life. Just as a little bit of yeast causes the whole lump of dough to puff up, so pride can distort all areas of church life.

> *"Just as Job was vindicated by God, so Paul hopes this wayward believer will be redeemed."*

5:7

"Get rid of the old yeast, so that you may be a new unleavened batch—as you really are. For Christ, our Passover lamb, has been sacrificed."

This analogy of yeast would have been an easy and clear illustration to the Corinthian believer. Yeast (or leaven) referred to a small lump of bread dough that could be traced back to the bread of years ago, bread that the people fed on and were sustained by. When this dough was folded into new dough it would have a big effect. Paul is calling the Corinthians to a fresh start, a break with the past. They were to feed on something new, and be influenced by a different agent of change. The reference to the Passover would have inevitably taken the Corinthians' minds to the Exodus, where God's people were set free from their bondage to slavery. Jews observed the Feast of unleavened bread, remembering that the Lord brought their divisions out of Egypt. For seven days no leaven was to be found in their homes: they needed a fresh start (Exo 12v17, 19).

5:8

"Therefore let us keep the Festival, not with the old bread leavened with malice and wickedness, but with the unleavened bread of sincerity and truth."

Paul has in mind here the Passover Festival: remembrance of salvation, of rescue from slavery into freedom. The believers' old way of life, with its cruel slave masters, was long gone; the old yeast of malice and wickedness is now firmly behind them - or, it should be. And yet, it is common knowledge that sexual immorality is present in their church, and they are proud of the fact! Paul argues that in light of the freedom they have, and the pervasive nature of sin (symbolised by the effect of the yeast on dough), they should act upon this situation. Sin will silently spread its destructive consequences throughout the congregation if left unchecked. If they feast on the bread of life (John 6v35), and His diet of sincerity and truth, He will give them an appetite for holiness and purity.

> *"They were to feed on something new, and be influenced by a different agent of change."*

5:9-10 | *"I wrote to you in my letter not to associate with sexually immoral people— not at all meaning the people of this world who are immoral, or the greedy and swindlers, or idolaters. In that case you would have to leave this world."*

Paul must have written a previous letter telling the Corinthians not to associate with sexually immoral people within the church, but somehow they misunderstood this. It seems they thought they were to withdraw from all those who didn't follow Christ - which was effectively most of the inhabitants of their city. That conclusion makes no sense to Paul; the citizens of Corinth needed to hear the message the church heralded. So the believers needed to draw close to the immoral, the greedy, the swindlers and the idolaters in Corinth. But they were to withdraw from those within the church who profess to follow Christ but continue to live sexually immoral lives.

> *"They were to withdraw from those within the church who profess to follow Christ but continue to live sexually immoral lives."*

5:11 | *"But now I am writing to you that you must not associate with anyone who claims to be a brother or sister but is sexually immoral or greedy, an idolater or slanderer, a drunkard or swindler. Do not even eat with such people."*

The issue Paul is addressing here is flagrant, unrepentant sin by a professing Christian. While Paul wants this person ultimately to be redeemed (5v5), he also wants this young church to be distinct. So he calls them not to associate with any believer who has ongoing, unrepentant sin in their lives - especially of the type that doesn't happen even among the Pagans (5v1). For someone to eat in your home meant they came under your protection and blessing; it was an expression of accepting and identifying with them. To do so with a follower of Jesus who pursues a sexually immoral lifestyle is untenable. Notice that most - if not all - of us are included in this catch-all list. Who does not commit idolatry (put something or somebody other than God as a source of satisfaction, purpose or meaning) at some point in a week? But a distinction should be made between sinning (falling short in specific things) and an ongoing unrepentant heart and lifestyle.

5:12-13

"What business is it of mine to judge those outside the church? Are you not to judge those inside? God will judge those outside. 'Expel the wicked person from among you.'"

While this may be uncomfortable reading to modern ears, judgement on God's people by God's people is not a new idea. Deuteronomy records that those among God's people who serve and worship other gods should be judged by God's people, and the evil purged from their midst (Deu 17 v6-7). God's people are to look out for one another, to preserve our distinct holiness, and this requires that we judge one another. But we are not to judge those outside of the household of God: He Himself will do that. Paul is not calling for the horror of the killing fields of the Khymer Rouge, where children and neighbours reported one another. Nor is he encouraging gossip or character assignation. Rather, he argues for a household set apart for God, who pursue holiness with zeal. Paul is painting a picture of a community who caringly call one another to lifestyles that reflect the holiness of God.

"God's people are to look out for one another, to preserve our distinct holiness, and this requires that we judge one another."

CHAPTER 6

6:1 | *"If any of you has a dispute with another, do you dare to take it before the ungodly for judgement instead of before the Lord's people?"*

Paul turns his attention to another concern: the Corinthian believers are taking out lawsuits against one another. You couldn't make this stuff up! Without a doubt, the Corinthian church was a melting pot of people and needed their father in Christ to bring some order. Some of these believers were still thinking of their old citizenship and its own ways of resolving conflict and finding justice. Fallen, sinful people will inevitably offend and grieve one another, regardless of whether they follow Christ or not. Jesus taught his disciples how to handle a brother or sister who has sinned against you (Matthew 18v15-17). The issue is not that members of the church disagree or have a dispute, but that they look to the ungodly to deliver justice rather than to God's people.

> *"Fallen, sinful people will inevitably offend and grieve one another, regardless of whether they follow Christ or not."*

6:2 | *"Or do you not know that the Lord's people will judge the world? And if you are to judge the world, are you not competent to judge trivial cases?"*

Some in the church had wronged each other in various ways, and instead of following Jesus' teaching recorded in Matthew 18v15-17, they turned to local magistrates. Paul is incredulous. Didn't they know they will participate with Christ in the final Day of Judgement? Had they forgotten this, or were they unaware of it? Jesus told his twelve disciples that they would "sit on thrones judging the twelve tribes of Israel" (Luke 22v30, Matt 19v28). The Apostle John saw thrones on which were seated 'those who had been given authority to judge; (Rev 20v4). Paul applies these teachings by Jesus to the wider church community. Somehow, all who follow Jesus - not just the twelve disciples - will participate in the judgement of eternal destiny and just reward. And if they are to participate in these ultimate judgements, then they are competent to judge the relatively trivial worldly matters about which they disagree.

6:3

> *"Do you not know that we will judge angels? How much more the things of this life!"*

Despite their divisions, sexual immorality, and lawsuits, Paul still sees who the Corinthians are in Christ. They have been enriched in every way (1v5), and will participate in the great day of judgement. All men and women throughout history will be judged by Christ, and somehow Christians will play a part in that. Followers of Christ will, in a meaningful way, judge the angels. The nature of angelic judgement is not clear; it may refer only to those who rebelled alongside Satan. What is clear is that Paul wants the Corinthians to act now in light of their future. If they are to judge mighty angelic beings, then they are qualified to judge more trivial cases in this life! Followers of Christ have the Holy Spirit within them. The Spirit equips and gives wisdom, and the spiritual man or woman can therefore make judgements about all things (2v15).

> *"What is clear is that Paul wants the Corinthians to act now in light of their future."*

6:4-5

> *"Therefore, if you have disputes about such matters, do you ask for a ruling from those whose way of life is scorned in the church? I say this to shame you. Is it possible that there is nobody among you wise enough to judge a dispute between believers?"*

Paul uses a rhetorical question to make his point: The answer is 'yes', they have foolishly asked for a ruling from someone with no standing in the church. Such is his strength of feeling on the issue that Paul wants to bring shame upon them. Despite the Corinthians feeling able to assess and select apostles, claiming "I follow Paul, I follow Apollos, I follow Cephas" (1v12), they still needed magistrates to settle trivial disputes. Without a doubt, they had the means within the church to settle these themselves. Paul cannot conceive the notion that there is no one sufficiently equipped or wise enough amongst them. Quite why the way of life of local magistrates is scorned in the church, is not clear, but the overall point remains the same.

6:6

> *"But instead, one brother takes another to court—and this in front of unbelievers!"*

Paul's concern is more than just unity amongst believers; he is also aware that unbelievers are 'reading' the church. Divisions within the church over apostles would largely be hidden to a watching world, but now their disagreements are being paraded to the local magistrates. God chose the foolish things to shame the wise (1v27), but these believers are bringing shame on themselves! They are not perfectly united in mind and thought (1v10), and they have legal documents and magistrates to testify to it. The phrase "and this in front of unbelievers" - or, in the ESV, "that before unbelievers" - evokes an image of a stage and an audience. The drama being played out is one of familiar disputes: a mundane courtroom drama with no surprises twists. The gallery look on, but there is nothing out of the ordinary; the Christians seem no different from everybody else.

6:7

> *"The very fact that you have lawsuits among you means you have been completely defeated already. Why not rather be wronged? Why not rather be cheated?"*

The lawsuits are yet another symptom of the Corinthians' ongoing arrogance. Whereas Christ - their great example - suffered wrongs for the greater good, these supposed followers were pursuing justification by unbelievers. While Christ submitted to a sentence of death, they look to magistrates to vindicate them. And whereas Christ was raised to victory, they are completely defeated. For the sake of the gospel and the unity of the church, Paul calls the Corinthians to endure being wronged. It is better to be cheated and trust God for vindication than to expose a Christian's fault before the courts. (Exceptions to this would be cases of abuse such as domestic, sexual or child abuse which should be reported). It is God who vindicates: He gives and He takes away, all is His and is for Him. It is better to be wronged than to bring the gospel into disrepute. God is our judge, and we are to exercise faith when we are wronged, trusting in God to vindicate us.

> *"It is better to be cheated and trust God for vindication than to expose a Christian's fault before the courts."*

6:8

"Instead, you yourselves cheat and do wrong, and you do this to your brothers and sisters."

Welcome to church! The believers in Corinth, who were sanctified in Christ and called to be holy (1v2), also defrauded one another. Local magistrates knew all about them because they were tasked with untangling some of their unethical practices. This is not the reputation Paul would want for the church - not to mention the damage that must have been caused to their own sense of fellowship. Worse still, victims became perpetrators: those who had been cheated or defrauded also then cheated and defrauded! The spiral continued; it seems to have become a normal part of the Corinthian church culture. In this area they are already defeated: they cheat and are cheated, they wrong and they are wronged. And they do this to their fellow believers in the church. Welcome to church.

6:9-10

"Or do you not know that wrongdoers will not inherit the kingdom of God? Do not be deceived: neither the sexually immoral nor idolaters nor adulterers nor men who have sex with men nor thieves nor the greedy nor drunkards nor slanderers nor swindlers will inherit the kingdom of God."

Paul uses irony and humour here to bring home his point. Not many of the Corinthians were wise, influential or noble, yet now they boast like kings. They have become haughty, like a well-established king who reigns with great riches. The result of their woefully deficient understanding of grace is a transformation in their opinion of themselves from 'nobodies' to 'mighty kings'. Paul teases them by playing along, wishing he could join them in reigning in their 'mighty kingship'. They consider themselves special, wise and worthy because they have forgotten that they received everything as a gift. These Corinthian 'kings' are quick to herald their assessments and opinions, yet their only real reason for boasting is Christ (1v31).

> *"There is a connection between what people profess, how they live, and what they receive from God when they die."*

6:11

> *"And that is what some of you were. But you were washed, you were sanctified, you were justified in the name of the Lord Jesus Christ and by the Spirit of our God."*

Some of the Corinthian believers were formally thieves, adulterers, drunkard and greedy. All of the Corinthians were sinners by other means. Yet that was not to be the defining act of their life.

They were washed: This refers to spiritual cleansing through faith in Christ. Their soiled and stained lives were washed clean, and all their guilt and shame removed. This was symbolised in their water baptism.

They were sanctified: This is a similar concept but has the sense of being set apart for a holy purpose. They have been prepared, and are being prepared, for service for God and therefore are to live a distinct lifestyle.

They were justified: God has already declared the Corinthian believers to be righteous. The righteousness that belonged to Christ has become theirs. The Corinthians need to live out a lifestyle consistent with this verdict and status.

"There can be a huge gulf between what is permissible and what is beneficial."

6:12

> *" 'I have the right to do anything,' you say—but not everything is beneficial. 'I have the right to do anything'—but I will not be mastered by anything."*

There can be a huge gulf between what is permissible and what is beneficial. You can feast on laxatives, but there will be consequences. Those who have been set apart as holy by the Spirit, and justified by the Christ, still need to exercise wisdom in their new found spiritual freedom. The requirements of God's holy law have been met by Christ, therefore no food or activity or craving can disqualify our right standing before God. Yet Paul reminds the church that the cravings of their bodies are tainted. What we associate with that food, activity or craving may be harmful to our soul or our sense of wholeness and well being. We can all too easily let sin master us again - and it desires to do so (Gen 4v7). Sin will use our freedom and cravings as a vehicle to enslave us.

6:13

> *"You say, 'Food for the stomach and the stomach for food, and God will destroy them both.' The body, however, is not meant for sexual immorality but for the Lord, and the Lord for the body."*

Here is another of the Corinthians' pithy phrases justifying themselves. In effect they are saying that gluttony is not a problem and can be enjoyed because God will ultimately renew everything. Yet Paul reminds them that the body's desires and cravings are to be met with reverence to its Creator and Lord. The believer's body is now the dwelling place of God: it is a temple of the Holy Spirit. It matters how we satisfy our bodies' God-given desires. The appetite for food is not be over-indulged; Christ alone is sufficient to bring comfort. Sexual appetites are to be satisfied within heterosexual marriage; that alone honours God. The physical body of a believer is joined and dedicated to Christ. The body is for the Lord; our body is His body (Eph 2v23). Therefore, gluttony and sexual immorality should be unthinkable. The Corinthians are joined to Christ, so they should should act accordingly.

"It matters how we satisfy our bodies' God-given desires."

6:14

> *"By his power God raised the Lord from the dead, and he will raise us also."*

Jesus' resurrection was the first; the mass resurrection of God's people is to follow. Just as God's power raised Jesus from death with an eternal body, so God will use that same power to raise all believers and give us eternal bodies. The point Paul is making is that our bodies are meant for the Lord, and are valuable to Him; therefore, He will raise them from the dead. Paul is making a link in his readers' minds between their mortal bodies and their resurrected bodies. He wants them to see that it matters what they do with the perishable seed because it will be sown, and then raised as imperishable (15v42-44). There is something of the believer's body that is valuable and will last eternally, so Paul urges the Corinthians to pursue holiness in everything they do with their bodies.

6:15

"Do you not know that your bodies are members of Christ himself? Shall I then take the members of Christ and unite them with a prostitute? Never!"

Some within the Corinthian church were having sex with prostitutes. This might seem shocking to the modern reader, but it was a common practice given their context of ritual sex as a form of idol worship. We satisfy our appetites for food by eating; they satisfied their hunger for sex by using the services of a prostitute. Yet Paul sees the church as Christ's body (Eph 1v23), and to unite Christ with sexual immorality is untenable: it must never happen. The revulsion Paul feels is about associating Christ with sexual immorality; it does not mean that prostitutes cannot believe, be forgiven, and belong to Christ. It is the act of uniting or associating Christ with sexual immorality that is abhorrent - not a prostitute in themself.

6:16-17

"Do you not know that he who unites himself with a prostitute is one with her in body? For it is said, 'The two will become one flesh.' But whoever is united with the Lord is one with him in spirit."

There is something mystical about sexual intercourse; it is more than a simple act of procreation or pleasure. Sex is also a metaphor for a much greater union between Christ and His church. It is part of what it means to be image-bearers betrothed to a faithful God. Regrettably, in many, if not all cultures, sex has been reduced to - at best - a desire for pleasure, or at worst merely an appetite to be met. With such a low view of sex, it matters little whether it was with a prostitute. Paul reminds the Corinthians that sex was designed by God as an expression of covenant unity between husband and wife. Their lifelong oneness is to be consummated in an act of love and pleasure. And this is an echo of a greater unity between Christ and His bride, the church. Sex between husband and wife points to the spiritual unity of the believer with their true Saviour and greater husband. Sexual immorality distorts, corrupts and obscures these truths.

> *"It is the act of uniting or associating Christ with sexual immorality that is abhorrent - not a prostitute in themself."*

6:18

> *"Flee from sexual immorality. All other sins a person commits are outside the body, but whoever sins sexually, sins against their own body."*

The Corinthians are to flee from sexual immorality. Flee means to run away from a place or situation of danger, to make a quick exit or get away. Paul urges the believers to flee, rather than to try to resist or to stand firm. These are wise words. Our sexual appetites can be very powerful, and can lead to damage - both to ourselves and to our relationship with our true and greater husband. Sexual activity outside of marriage is a unique sin in that it is both against Christ and against our own bodies. Paul's audience are not to flee sex within marriage - it is to be enjoyed by husband and wife with thanksgiving. But sexual activity outside of marriage is incompatible with following Christ.

> *"Christians are the dwelling place of the Holy Spirit; we must live in a manner that reflects the privilege of being indwelt by God Himself."*

6:19

> *"Do you not know that your bodies are temples of the Holy Spirit, who is in you, whom you have received from God? You are not your own;"*

The meeting place of God and His people had always been a temple: first the garden temple of Eden, then the Tabernacle Tent, and lastly the glorious temple built by Solomon. Access to the garden temple was forfeited (Gen 3v24), and subsequent temples were superseded or torn down. But now a new temple has been established. All those who follow Christ become the temple of the Holy Spirit, a holy temple in the Lord (Eph 2v21), a dwelling in which God lives by His Spirit. Paul reminds these beloved Corinthians that they are indwelt by the Holy Spirit. The Jerusalem temple was once the dwelling place of God, it would have been highly inappropriate to have sex with a prostitute there. But now the dwelling place of God was within His people, how much more inappropriate for Christians to have sex with a prostitute. Christians are the dwelling place of the Holy Spirit; we must live in a manner that reflects the privilege of being indwelt by God Himself.

6:20

"you were bought at a price. Therefore honor God with your bodies."

Paul wrote to the church in Rome: "But thanks be to God that, though you used to be slaves to sin, you have come to obey from your heart the pattern of teaching that has now claimed your allegiance" (Rom 6v17). Again, here, he uses an image from the slave market: the Corinthians have been purchased at a great price. Their new Master demands to be honoured by how they conduct themselves; they are to act in a manner befitting the household they've joined. Paul reminds them that they have been bought at extraordinary cost, and with that comes a duty to honour God with their bodies. Temples of the Holy Spirit are not to be associated with sexual immorality. Slaves do their Master's bidding, and their Master calls them to righteous living. Those who were washed, sanctified and justified by their new Master are also are called to honour Him with how they use their bodies.

CHAPTER 7

7:1 | *"Now for the matters you wrote about: 'It is good for a man not to have sexual relations with a woman.'"*

Up to this point in the letter, Paul was responding to the verbal report given by some from Chloe's household (1v11). Now he turns his attention to answering questions the church asked in a previous letter - questions about sex, marriage, food sacrificed to idols, spiritual gifts, and a financial offering for needy Jewish Christians in Jerusalem. The first question raised was whether to refrain from sex within marriage. The Corinthian church was a hotbed for religious zeal and spiritual gifts. And within this fervour there there was some confusion around sexuality; specifically, some promoted abstinence from marital intimacy. Bearing in mind the highly sexualized culture in Corinth, this raised some concerns, so they asked Paul for his advice.

> *"They are to meet each other's needs, guarding one another against sexual immorality and temptation."*

7:2 | *"But since sexual immorality is occurring, each man should have sexual relations with his own wife, and each woman with her own husband."*

You can almost hear Paul's mind organising his thoughts as he makes a series of statements. He places his theology within a pragmatic response by acknowledging the context of sexual immorality, both outside and inside the church. Ritual sex was practiced in their city, church members slept with prostitutes (6v16), and a believer even slept with his father's wife (5v1). Paul acknowledges both their environment and their libidos. He concludes it is better for them to be married, and that spouses should meet each other's God-given appetites. Paul makes the point that each wife should also have her desires met; there is to be sexual equality between men and women. Husbands and wives are to be monogamous and faithful. They are to meet each other's needs, guarding one another against sexual immorality and temptation.

7:3

"The husband should fulfill his marital duty to his wife, and likewise the wife to her husband."

Paul speaks of sexual intercourse as a marital duty; both husband and wife have an obligation and a responsibility to fulfil. Whilst this may seem clinical - sexual intimacy reduced to function - the principle is commitment to the marriage covenant. In a society where sexual immorality is prevalent, Paul urges spouses to look to and look out for one another. Sexual needs are to be met and satisfied within marriage. Husbands and wives have an obligation and expectation to meet, based on their love for God and for one another. Neither spouse should withhold nor minimise this; sex is good and sexual desire is an appropriate appetite, which is to be met by your spouse. A Christian's body is not meant for sexual immorality but for the Lord. Likewise, a married person's body is not their own, but belongs to their spouse. Both husband and wife should make themselves available to their spouse if she or he desires intercourse. This is a principle to be outworked, not a command.

> "The antidote to sexual immorality is to give your body to your spouse, rather than to refrain from marital intimacy."

7:4

"The wife does not have authority over her own body but yields it to her husband. In the same way, the husband does not have authority over his own body but yields it to his wife."

In Christian marriage, spouses willingly agree to give their body to each other. It is no longer theirs alone, but in love and trust they yield it to their spouse. Ownership is not transferred, but now another can also lay claim to it. When we give our body to our spouse they are blessed and benefit from this exclusive gift. The husband does not own his wife's body, nor is her body something to be used. Rather her body is given in trust, as her investment in their 'one flesh' union. So, too, the husband, no longer has the sole authority over his body: his wife can now lay claim to it. Paul writes that the antidote to sexual immorality is to give your body to your spouse, rather than to refrain from marital intimacy. Spouses are encouraged to "drink water from your own cistern, running water from your own well" (Pro 5v15).

7:5

"Do not deprive each other except perhaps by mutual consent and for a time, so that you may devote yourselves to prayer. Then come together again so that Satan will not tempt you because of your lack of self-control."

In Paul's mind, ongoing sexual union is the norm for married life. However, he concedes that husband and wife can - by mutual agreement - decide to abstain for a set period of time in order to devote themselves to prayer. A fast from sexual intimacy can be a helpful way of harnessing unmet appetites in order to pursue God in prayer. Whilst this is permissible, he reminds the believers that they have both a weakness and an enemy. Satan will exploit their lack of self-control, and so they should be sure to come back together for intimacy after the agreed time. All areas of our lives are to come under the Lordship of Christ; no appetite is beyond his headship. Our identity is in Christ: he alone is sufficient, and we are weak. Husband and wife resist temptation by celebrating their unity through sexual intimacy.

7:6-7

"I say this as a concession, not as a command. I wish that all of you were as I am. But each of you has your own gift from God; one has this gift, another has that."

The concession Paul speaks of here is agreeing to abstain from sex to pursue intense prayer. This should only be for an agreed time because Satan will endeavour to hijack their unmet sexual appetite and their lack of self control. His concern is what might happen due to their unmet sexual appetites and their lack of self control (v5). He writes: "I wish that all men were as I am". Given the immediate context of v5 (temptation and self control) this most likely refers to Paul's well-developed sense of self-control, which is a fruit of the Spirit (Gal 5v23). It is worth noting that he does not command them to abstain. His thinking seems to be that to fast from sexual intimacy in order to devote themselves to prayer is a good practice. Yet he acknowledges that their hunger in this area may well grow beyond their limits of self-control. It is worth quickly noting that, whilst Jesus remained unmarried and yet was fulfilled, the Bible consistently affirms that sex within marriage is not only permissible but is good and to be enjoyed.

> *"To fast from sexual intimacy in order to devote themselves to prayer is a good practice."*

7:8-9

"Now to the unmarried and the widows I say: It is good for them to stay unmarried, as I do. But if they cannot control themselves, they should marry, for it is better to marry than to burn with passion."

Both marriage and singleness (celibacy) have their own benefits. While marriage will be the normal expectation for most people (driven by a God given desire for lifelong companionship and to raise children), Paul notices and affirms those who are unmarried. He has observed that those who marry face many troubles in this life (v28), and he wants to spare them from this. Yet he is also aware of the sexualized culture at Corinth; a seaport would have been well served by prostitutes. Paul is revealing his pragmatic approach to Christian living; the pursuit of holy living has multiple paths. These include deciding whether to marry, or not, purely on the basis of one's sexual appetite and measure of self-control. Whilst it may seem scandalous to marry to have a libido satisfied, it is more preferable than pursuing sexual immorality. Temples of the Holy Spirit are to be kept holy. It is better to marry than to unite Christ to acts of sexual immorality with a prostitute (6v15).

7:10-11

"To the married I give this command (not I, but the Lord): A wife must not separate from her husband. But if she does, she must remain unmarried or else be reconciled to her husband. And a husband must not divorce his wife."

Paul charges the Corinthian believers to stay married. The wife should not separate from her husband, and the husband should not divorce his wife. He urges them to obey Jesus' teaching on this subject: "What God has joined together, let no one separate" and "I tell you that anyone who divorces his wife, except for sexual immorality, and marries another woman commits adultery" (Matt 19v6,9). Those who have believing spouses are commanded not to send them away. If they separate they must then remain unmarried, or else work for reconciliation. Paul conceives of a situation where a marriage has broken down to such a degree that it is pragmatic to live apart, but nonetheless the marriage will still stand. Roman law permitted either couple to initiate a divorce with no stated cause required; this is not the case with Jesus.

"The pursuit of holy living has multiple paths."

7:12

> "To the rest I say this (I, not the Lord): If any brother has a wife who is not a believer and she is willing to live with him, he must not divorce her."

The Greek culture of the day prioritised oral tradition. This is a form of communication where people recall and pass on specific information accurately through speech rather than writing. Much of the formation of the Gospels relied upon oral tradition, albeit helped by the Holy Spirit. Clearly the twelve apostles were not following Jesus with notepads, writing down every word He said. We can see Paul making use of this tradition in verse 10, since Matthew 19 hadn't yet been written for him to refer to. But Paul does not quote a Jesus teaching about where one spouse has converted and the other has not, presumably because he was unaware of any such specific instruction. So Paul gives signals that what he is about to say is from himself as an apostle of Christ Jesus (1v1). He applied Jesus' teaching in a way that is authoritative and binding, not merely as a suggestion. If an unbelieving wife is willing to stay with her believing husband, he must not divorce her.

> "Marriage is God's building block for society; both adults and children thrive in a stable home life."

7:13

> "And if a woman has a husband who is not a believer and he is willing to live with her, she must not divorce him."

Verses 12-13 set out Paul's expectation for husbands and wives who have unbelieving spouses: they must not divorce if their spouse is willing to live with them. The flow of the letter is addressing questions around sexual activity, immorality, marriage and divorce. Paul is affirming the marriage and union of husband and wife - even if one becomes a believer and the other remains unsaved. A believer's union to an unbelieving spouse does not defile them, nor does it bring into question their right standing before God. So long as their unbelieving spouse is willing to live with them, they must not divorce. Neither should they abstain from sexual union or be concerned for their holiness. Marriage is God's building block for society; both adults and children thrive in a stable home life.

7:14

> *"For the unbelieving husband has been sanctified through his wife, and the unbelieving wife has been sanctified through her believing husband. Otherwise your children would be unclean, but as it is, they are holy."*

On first reading, it would seem that holiness is transferrable rather than imputed (assigned, attributed). But this is not what Paul means. To be "sanctified", or made holy, is to be set apart. The unbelieving husband or wife is not saved through their union with their believing spouse, as verse 16 will later highlight. Rather, they are set apart from other unbelievers because of the Christian influence from their spouse. It is in that sense that they have been "sanctified". Believing spouses are not to withdraw from their unbelieving spouse and children for fear of being made unclean. Their loved ones are set apart sanctified because of the faith of the believer. The positive morale and spiritual influence of the believing parent outweighs the influence of the unbelieving parent.

> *"The positive morale and spiritual influence of the believing parent outweighs the influence of the unbelieving parent."*

7:15

> *"But if the unbeliever leaves, let it be so. The brother or the sister is not bound in such circumstances; God has called us to live in peace."*

Paul foresees situations in which the unbelieving spouse may be sympathetic or antagonistic. In the latter circumstance, Paul urges the believer to let them go: they are not bound to their unbelieving wife or husband. The Christian is not to try to manipulate reconciliation; they are to pursue peace, even if that means separation. The peace referred to here is the shalom of God, the sense of wellbeing and that "all is well". The ESV uses the phrase "the brother or sister is not enslaved". This speaks of release from binding obligations - maybe even freedom to pursue divorce and remarry. Whatever was in Paul's mind, what is clear is that a believer who is abandoned by their unbelieving spouse is not obligated to seek reconciliation but is called to live in peace.

7:16

"How do you know, wife, whether you will save your husband? Or, how do you know, husband, whether you will save your wife?"

Salvation belongs to God (Rev 7v10); He is the One who saves. The Holy Spirit is His agent, and we are the harvester (Matt 9v38). We can't save anyone - and yet we are witnesses and heralds of the good news. But we don't know who will get saved. In this context, Paul releases the abandoned believer from their concern for their spouse's salvation. Their Christian influence upon their estranged spouse is no guarantee that they would be saved. Rather, the believer is called to live in peace and to trust God for their estranged spouse. They must in faith in the goodness of God, relinquish the hope given in 1 Peter 3v1 that "husbands who do not obey the word may be won without a word by the conduct of their wives". Whilst the believer is a powerful witness, it is God alone who opens blind eyes and melts hard hearts.

7:17

"Nevertheless, each person should live as a believer in whatever situation the Lord has assigned to them, just as God has called them. This is the rule I lay down in all the churches."

Paul moves his thoughts to the believers' God-given vocation in life, the idea of following a particular career, service or lifestyle with a sense of divine calling. Paul suggests that each believer has a place in life "assigned" to them, a purpose to which God has called them. He will go on to express that purpose in terms of family, religious background, and economics. This is not optional thinking: it is a rule he lays down in all of the churches. When people are saved, they should not abandon their way of life, but look to embrace and redeem their present situation. Paul encourages the Corinthians to be confident that God has placed them in their particular situation for a purpose: to bring His Kingdom to bear.

"Whilst the believer is a powerful witness, it is God alone who opens blind eyes and melts hard hearts."

7:18-19

"Was a man already circumcised when he was called? He should not become uncircumcised. Was a man uncircumcised when he was called? He should not be circumcised. Circumcision is nothing and uncircumcision is nothing. Keeping God's commands is what counts."

The impact of a Jew calling circumcision "nothing" can be lost on the Gentile reader. Circumcision was the physical mark of God's covenant upon the Jewish man. Yet for the Christian church this practice was now obsolete; it had been superseded by the Holy Spirit as the seal of the new covenant (Eph 1v13). Circumcision now meant nothing, so there was no need for it to be continued, celebrated, or even reversed (a medical procedure called epispasm). What counts now is keeping God's commandments, obedience to God's new covenant in the teachings of Jesus and his apostles. Paul is teaching the Corinthian church what that obedience should look like.

7:20

"Each person should remain in the situation they were in when God called them."

Paul restates the rule he lays down in all the churches (v17); each person should retain the place in life that the Lord assigned them and called them to. Did God assign them a Jewish heritage? Then they should not renounce their cultural background and community - although faith in Christ is what counts. Are they married to an unbeliever? Are they willing to live with them? If so, they must not divorce. Christ's work of redemption transcends personal situations; His imputed righteousness is unaffected by our situations. Whilst our lifestyle choices and values will change enormously when we believe in Christ, we should remain where we were when God called us, confident that our 'assignment' is from God. The light of Christ shines out from wherever God has placed us in this broken world. This is the general rule - but there are exceptions.

"The light of Christ shines out from wherever God has placed us in this broken world."

7:21

> *"Were you a slave when you were called? Don't let it trouble you—although if you can gain your freedom, do so."*

To our modern ears, telling a slave not to be troubled by their bondage rightly seems crass and repugnant. To make sense of Paul's statement we need to remind ourselves of aspects of first century slavery. The Roman institution of bond servitude allowed for the servant to earn money, save, and buy their freedom. They were not only labourers but were often entrusted with significant responsibility. Once they had bought their freedom they were regarded as Roman freemen. Yet Paul does encourage such slaves to gain their freedom if they can. Elsewhere, the Bible does denounce slave traders (1 Tim 1v10; Rev 18v11-13), and affirms that all people are equal. Paul encourages the bond servant not to be concerned: they have a true master who has called them and laid down his life for them. He counsels slaves to trust God, to live quiet and peaceful lives, and to gain their freedom if possible (1 Thess 4v1).

> *"Remaining in the situation involves a complete shift in thinking, even if outwardly nothing changes."*

7:22

> *"For the one who was a slave when called to faith in the Lord is the Lord's freed person; similarly, the one who was free when called is Christ's slave."*

Paul presses home his thinking by illustrating what it means to follow Christ, both for a slave and a free person. The slave has gained a new master, the Lord. But He is not looking to hold anyone in spiritual bondage; rather, He bought them in order to release them into true freedom. Conversely, the one who was free has become a slave of righteousness. God has transformed their heart and they now long to be obedient: they become a slave to Christ's teaching. Remaining in the situation involves a complete shift in thinking, even if outwardly nothing changes. The slave has a new master and can regard himself a free man, but his new master says "retain your place in life". The free man must now consider himself a slave, but his new master says "remain in your situation".

7:23

"You were bought at a price; do not become slaves of human beings."

It is very difficult to grasp the high price paid to free people from slavery to Sin, Satan and Death. What was the cost to the Father to pour His wrath upon His innocent Son? What cost to the Son to be fully identified with the sins of those to be redeemed? What cost to the Spirit to restrain His own power and not act upon the Son's behalf? The redeemed have been bought at a truly high price. So Paul forbids a believer to sell themselves back into any form of slavery. This may seem obvious to us, but slavery was a common means of solving personal financial challenges. The Corinthian believers have a new master, who is both jealous and generous. He is a jealous God, who is like a good husband, and has no appetite to share his beloved with another. He is also well able to meet their needs, be that financial (He owns the cattle on a thousand hills Psa 50v10); or their need for approval and identity.

> *"Their 'Master' has set them free to live righteously, obediently, and joyfully."*

7:24

"Brothers and sisters, each person, as responsible to God, should remain in the situation they were in when God called them."

For the third time, Paul stresses that the Corinthians should remain in the situation God has given them (v17, 20). God is their Master; He has assigned them a place in life. They are to give an account to Him, and they should be obedient to His God's commands. Their 'Master' has set them free to live righteously, obediently, and joyfully. God has prepared good works for both the free person and the slave to do (Eph 2v10). These good works include both their domestic and employment situations. Whilst the slave should try to gain their freedom (v21), no one in the church should be troubled or proud. They are to think no more nor less of themselves whether they're married or single, circumcised or not, slave or free. All are called by God, all are answerable to Him, and all are to be obedient to Him.

7:25 | *"Now about virgins: I have no command from the Lord, but I give a judgement as one who by the Lord's mercy is trustworthy."*

Here we have another illustration of Paul's sense of calling, and his difference from Jesus' teaching. He is an apostle of Christ Jesus, whom he encountered near Damascus (Acts 9v5). As Jesus' delegate, Paul was quick to relay his actual words on any given subject (7v10 refers to Matthew 19v6). When Paul was unaware of Jesus' teaching he would state so (7v12), but these occasions do not mean that Paul is teaching with less authority. Paul is aware that it is by God's mercy, not by his own merit or eloquence, that he can give trustworthy judgements on subjects or answers to questions. Note, though, that Paul says he is trustworthy, not omniscient (all knowing). He is a faithful steward of the Gospel, not the all-knowing fount of God's wisdom. Paul turns his attention now to answering the Corinthians' question about those who were betrothed: people of marriageable age but had never married.

7:26-27 | *"Because of the present crisis, I think that it is good for a man to remain as he is. Are you pledged to a woman? Do not seek to be released. Are you free from such a commitment? Do not look for a wife."*

Paul speaks of a "present crisis", which could mean the pressure of living the last days (v29), or maybe famine or persecution (Acts 18v6). Whatever it is, he thinks it is best for the Corinthians to remain in their current marital status (v17, 20, 24). Paul recognises that they are living in difficult times, and starting married life in times of distress is not advisable. People should stay married or stay single; he advises against changing status. Neither is a more preferable option, given their state of crisis. The married have a spouse to comfort them, but also the added weight of concern for their partner's well being. The single have no companion to comfort them, but neither do they have the weight of concern for another. In times of crisis, being content in God and His sufficiency is of primary concern.

> *"He is a faithful steward of the Gospel, not the all-knowing fount of God's wisdom."*

7:28

"But if you do marry, you have not sinned; and if a virgin marries, she has not sinned. But those who marry will face many troubles in this life, and I want to spare you this."

Because of this present crisis (v26), Paul advises them to stay in the matrimonial state they are in. Getting married is not sinful or wrong, but given the situation it opens to the door to lots of worldly trouble. Marriage introduces another layer of complexity and responsibilities (which Paul refers to as "troubles") that he would want to spare them from. This may seem like a negative outlook on the institution of marriage, but in distressing times there is much to commend in this approach. Single people can serve Christ with wholehearted devotion, free from other demands, as both Jesus and Paul demonstrated. The Christian tradition of monks and nuns is a great example of this devotion and wisdom. Paul wishes that all of the Corinthians were as free to be devoted to Christ as he is, yet and he recognises that being content to be single is a gift from God (v7).

7:29

"What I mean, brothers and sisters, is that the time is short. From now on those who have wives should live as if they do not;"

What does Paul mean when he writes that "time is short"? The natural reading of the next few verses suggests that he was expecting Christ to return in the next few weeks or months. He seems to be saying that Christ is coming so live as though you weren't married: give yourselves fully to God's Kingdom. The whole purpose of Paul's letter is to let the Corinthians know how to do 'normal life' and the 'daily affairs' of following Christ in the bustling and troubled seaport that is their home. From Paul's other writings it is clear that he considers the time from the resurrection to the second coming as the 'last days'. So they are to live in the anticipation of Christ's return, at an hour they cannot predict (Matt 24v44). In that sense they are to live with a sense of urgency, as though time is short. We, too, are to live with a sense of urgency, for Christ is returning soon.

> *"We, too, are to live with a sense of urgency, for Christ is returning soon."*

7:30-31

"those who mourn, as if they did not; those who are happy, as if they were not; those who buy something, as if it were not theirs to keep; those who use the things of the world, as if not engrossed in them. For this world in its present form is passing away."

Paul is not arguing for a flat, emotionless Christian life. He is not advocating for zero expressions of joy or sadness, of ownership or passion. Rather, he wants the Corinthians to see 'mourning' in light of all things being renewed, 'happiness' in light of all things being renewed, etc... The things of this world - things that make us happy or sad, the stuff we buy, use and enjoy - are all temporary. Even the present crisis (v26), and the many troubles that married people face (v28), are passing away. As such, those who follow Jesus should regard their relationships with people and possessions accordingly. This world in its present form is passing away. But it will be renewed, and whoever does the will of God abides forever (1 John 2v17).

> ## *"He is single and content, and wishes that others could be as he is."*

7:32-33

"I would like you to be free from concern. An unmarried man is concerned about the Lord's affairs—how he can please the Lord. But a married man is concerned about the affairs of this world—how he can please his wife—"

Paul's message is clear: living as a single person has distinct advantages, not least allowing him a razor sharp focus on the Lord's affairs. Paul is not saying that it is wrong to be married or to be concerned for your spouse. He wrote to the church in Ephesus that husbands are to love their wives as Christ loves the church (Eph 5v25). But he acknowledges that marriage divides your interests and multiplies your concerns. He is single and content, and wishes that others could be as he is. He exemplified single-minded devotion; hardship and setbacks were his constant companions on his travels (2 Cor 11v23-29). He faced daily pressure and responsibility for the churches he cared for. Being wholly concerned about the Lord's affairs was no easy alternative to marriage, but his attention was not divided.

7:34

> "and his interests are divided. An unmarried woman or virgin is concerned about the Lord's affairs: Her aim is to be devoted to the Lord in both body and spirit. But a married woman is concerned about the affairs of this world—how she can please her husband."

Paul's assumptions for single people are wholly different to ours. We tend to see singleness as a life stage. The teens and twenties are a time for enjoying life, and pursuing a career or pleasure before the responsibilities (and restrictions) of marriage and children. This means that, singleness in midlife is seen as undesirable, as though somehow such people they have missed the boat. Paul sees it very differently: to him, singleness is a gift because you can devote yourself wholeheartedly to the Lord. He sees it as entirely plausible to live and thrive without being married. The single woman is free to give all her time and energy, body and spirit, to God. She does not have to divide nor to feel conflicted. We see here the roots of the nuns and monks of the Christian tradition: people who take Paul's words seriously, embracing singleness with the aim of being devoted to the Lord.

> "He is not trying to control or restrict them, but to help them live in undivided devotion to Christ."

7:35

> "I am saying this for your own good, not to restrict you, but that you may live in a right way in undivided devotion to the Lord."

Paul has the heart of a spiritual father (4v15) and wants good for the Corinthian church, to free them from concerns and anxieties. He is not trying to control or restrict them, but to help them live in undivided devotion to Christ. For Paul, devotion to Christ is all benefit: it is highly desirable and advantageous. He wants to help his spiritual children make good choices. Undivided devotion to the Lord will have many faces: for Paul it was living as a single man. That way, he could concern himself solely with reaching the Gentiles and caring for churches. While few are called to that, all of us are called to live in an orderly way that secures our undivided devotion to Christ. And this, of course is all benefit and advantage to us.

7:36 | *"If anyone is worried that he might not be acting honorably toward the virgin he is engaged to, and if his passions are too strong and he feels he ought to marry, he should do as he wants. He is not sinning. They should get married."*

Sometimes the Bible is surprisingly frank and practical. Paul has laid out a case for staying single in order to be devoted to the Lord. However, there is much sexual immorality in Corinth, which arouses strong passions in all, including in single people. So spouses are encouraged to fulfil their marital duties, guarding themselves against sexual temptation. Paul tells single people who have little or no self-control to marry rather than to burn with sexual passion. But what is not clear is what this reference to "not acting honourably'" means. Presumably it doesn't refer to sexual sin, otherwise Paul would have denounced it. Most likely we will never know. What is clear is that an engaged man or woman is free to marry, even though Paul has stated the case for single-minded devotion to Jesus. The God-given appetite for sex may grow too strong for some, and they are free to marry.

7:37 | *"But the man who has settled the matter in his own mind, who is under no compulsion but has control over his own will, and who has made up his mind not to marry the virgin—this man also does the right thing."*

This whole chapter started with quoting the Corinthians' letter: "It is good for a man not to have sexual relations with a woman". Paul returns now to this idea, but with qualifying words. The engaged man or woman can choose not to marry, so long as they are not being compelled by others. Paul underlines the conviction required to pursue and persist in celibacy. Those who choose to break off an engagement must be firmly established in heart and have their sexual desires under control. The man or woman who has made up their mind not to marry does well, even though they will upset and disappoint another. They have chosen a greater thing: to fully devote themselves to the concerns of the Lord.

> *"What is clear is that an engaged man or woman is free to marry, even though Paul has stated the case for single-minded devotion to Jesus."*

7:38
"So then, he who marries the virgin does right, but he who does not marry her does better."

It's difficult to know whether singleness is Paul's personal preference for himself or his ideal for everyone. Either way, it is good to note that not all choices carry a binary moral outcome (right or wrong). The choice here is between "right" or "better", and depends on your personal gift from God. Knowing who you are and what you want and need in life is helpful when faced with morally neutral but significant choices. In this instance, those who are self-controlled and settled in their heart do better to remain single; they can be devoted to God in the present difficult circumstances. But those who will most likely 'burn' with passion do right in getting married, even though their interests will be divided and their troubles multiplied (v28). For Paul, who received the gift of self-control for singleness (v7), the better choice is clear. Paul knew who he was. The question for us is, do we?

7:39
"A woman is bound to her husband as long as he lives. But if her husband dies, she is free to marry anyone she wishes, but he must belong to the Lord."

Paul switches now to addressing the widows, concluding his answer on the question the Corinthians raised about marriage (v1). Husband and wife are bound to each other until one of them dies. This verse, when linked to verses 10 and 11, is a powerful argument against divorce amongst believers. These verses are to be taken seriously, even if they don't constitute the full New Testament teaching on marriage and divorce (see also Matt 5v32, 19v8-12). Just as the church is bound to Jesus, so is the wife bound to her husband (Eph 5v32) until death.

But while death ends the marriage covenant between husband and wife, mercifully the same is not true for Jesus and the church.

After the death of a spouse, a widower is free to remarry whoever they desire - so long as the new partner is a Christian.

> *"Knowing who you are and what you want and need in life is helpful when faced with morally neutral but significant choices."*

7:40

"In my judgement, she is happier if she stays as she is—and I think that I too have the Spirit of God."

Paul concludes by saying that widowers would be happier focusing solely on the Lord's affairs. They are free to remarry a believer, but in his opinion, they would be happier remaining single. Paul then adds the curious phrase "I think that I too have the Spirit of God". This must be his way of adding weight to this judgement; Paul is speaking not as a bitter single man, but as one who is full of joy in the Holy Spirit, entrusted with the secret things of God (1v1, 4v1). He confidently calls the unmarried and widows to stay as they are, just as he is doing (v8). Those who are full of the Holy Spirit are able to control their sexual passion and know great contentment in service to God. Those who have the Spirit of God are not defined by marriage, singleness, or sexual activity, but all are called to devotion to the Lord's affairs.

> *"Paul is speaking not as a bitter single man, but as one who is full of joy in the Holy Spirit, entrusted with the secret things of God."*

CHAPTER 8

8:1 | *"Now about food sacrificed to idols: we know that we all possess knowledge. Knowledge puffs up, but love builds up."*

Paul moves to the Corinthians' question about food used in religious services. Many animals were sacrificed daily in Corinth's numerous temples as acts of worship to the various deities. The selling, buying and eating of food sacrificed to idols was common: pagan sacrifices would not use all of the animal and so the unused portions would either be sold in the market or used in a dining hall attached to the temple. This practice raised a few questions from this young church. The ESV places quotation marks around the phrase "all of us possess knowledge", implying it to be a quote from the Corinthians' letter. So Paul begins by stating that knowledge can breed arrogance. This is something he has already highlighted as a concern (see boasting in 3v21, pride in 4v6, and arrogance in 4v18-19).

"Knowledge dispensed with love is a blessing to all."

8:2 | *"The man who thinks he knows something does not yet know as he ought to know."*

Paul is laying the foundation for his answer by exploring the relationship between knowledge and love. Knowledge puffs up, but love builds up. The person who 'imagines' they know something really hasn't gotten to the heart of true understanding. Here, then, is the challenge of learning: to stay humble while growing knowledgeable; to think much, but always for the good of others. Facts without love create a sterile vacuum that chokes life. Knowledge with love is a fertile field. True understanding is only expressed in the currency of love. When love and knowledge are inseparable the people are glad. After all, God is both all knowing and is Love. Knowledge dispensed with love is a blessing to all. Knowledge without love is at best clumsy; at worst, it is destructive arrogance.

8:3 | *"But the man who loves God is known by God."*

Paul contrasts the arrogance of the person who thinks they 'know something' with the person who loves God. The one who loves God is also known by God. God knows their failings and their shortfalls, their strength and their weakness. God knows this, and yet chooses to relate to them in love and mercy. When knowledge puffs you up, you don't yet know as you ought to know. The one who loves God is known and loved by God. This builds up a believer; it should not puff them up.

> *"Idols have no life to give, they only take on that life which their worshippers give them."*

8:4 | *"So then, about eating food sacrificed to idols: we know that an idol is nothing at all in the world and that there is no God but one."*

Paul starts his answer by addressing the mature in Christ - those who 'love God and are known by God' - and will then contrast this with an address to newer believers (v4-6, v7). He affirms that idols are nothing, and there is only one God, presumably in response to some of the statements in their original letter (hence quotation marks in the ESV). He affirms that an idol has no real existence; it is counterfeit and need not be feared, nor acknowledged with reverence. Idols exist in a physical sense, in that they are images made of wood, stone, silver or gold (Deu 29v17). But they are only that. Idols have no life to give, they only take on that life which their worshippers give them. Sadly, we often allow idols to entrap our hearts even though they are poor substitutes that can deliver neither life nor hope.

8:5

> *"For even if there are so-called gods, whether in heaven or on earth (as indeed there are many 'gods' and many 'lords'),"*

Any short walk around the city would pass shrines and temples to the various "gods" and "lords" of Corinth. Take your pick, choose a god, the choice is yours: there is one on every corner! They were an ever-present testimony of the "many lords" of the great city. Paul acknowledges this, despite him regarding these objects as nothing in and of themselves. They are merely created things, constructs of people's hopes, fears and imaginations. Yet they were an undeniable thread of the fabric of Corinthian culture - hence the Corinthians' question about eating food sacrificed to them. You couldn't easily escape their influence. But there is no substance to their reality; they were gods and lords in name only. Calling something "god" does not make it so.

8:6

> *"yet for us there is but one God, the Father, from whom all things came and for whom we live; and there is but one Lord, Jesus Christ, through whom all things came and through whom we live."*

In a dramatic contrast to the idols, that are nothing, Paul reminds his readers of the central role of the Father and Son on planet earth. The Father is the source and the goal; the Son is the means and the mediator. Both are one in purpose. The Father is the benevolent initiator, from whom and for whom we exist. All things came from Him; He is the supreme being for whom we exist. The Son is the Lord, through whom all things exist. By him all things were created, in heaven and on earth, and He holds all things together (Col 1v16-17). It is through Christ that we live. He is our Lord and Master, and the means of grace and life to us. It is with this expansive view of God that Paul answers the church's questions about eating meat offered to idols.

> *"The Father is the source and the goal; the Son is the means and the mediator."*

8:7

"But not everyone possesses this knowledge. Some people are still so accustomed to idols that when they eat sacrificial food they think of it as having been sacrificed to a god, and since their conscience is weak, it is defiled."

Paul began by stating that "we know an idol is nothing at all", but he now acknowledges that "not everyone knows this". Some believers in the Corinth church had a long and personal history of idol worship. They still vividly remember their old way of life, with its rituals and false hopes. So, now, when they eat food used in worship at pagan temples they feel defiled, as though their spiritual purity has been spoilt or degraded. Whilst food can't rob anyone of their right standing before God the Father, it might unsettle believers or rob them of a clear conscience. Our conscience is God-given, and helps us to follow Jesus in our daily choices. Our conscience needs both to be listened to and to be constantly informed by gospel truth.

8:8

"But food does not bring us near to God; we are no worse if we do not eat, and no better if we do".

For pagans, offering a food sacrifice was the means of drawing near to and appeasing their god. But for Christians, that goal has been supremely accomplished through faith in Christ Jesus. Food has no part to play in that. Paul reminds the Corinthians that eating meat sacrificed to idols or eating "all kinds of four-footed animals, as well as reptiles and birds of the air" (Acts 10v12) does not make them defiled, impure or unclean. Whatever enters the mouth goes into the stomach and then out of the body. It is the things that come out of the mouth from the heart that can make a person unclean (Matt 15v17). If the Corinthian believers eat food sacrificed to idols, they are no worse off than if they hadn't eaten it. The one who loves God is known by God, with their heart laid bare; still, God shows love and favour to them. The covenant sealed by Christ's blood is robust; it transcends things like food. It is faith in Christ that draws us near to God and gives us right standing before Him. Your stomach may or may not be full, but if you believe in Christ your righteousness is complete.

"Our conscience needs both to be listened to and to be constantly informed by gospel truth."

8:9 | *"Be careful, however, that the exercise of your rights does not become a stumbling block to the weak."*

Christian maturity is not just about knowing the right stuff; it has to include concern for the wellbeing of others. Paul urges the Corinthian believers to be careful that their knowledge and liberty does not confuse fellow believers. Exercising their freedom must not cause others to stumble. Paul has in mind those in the church who might struggle with their mature role-models eating food that has been used in temple worship. Those who consider themselves mature in their faith are to put the needs of spiritually younger brothers and sisters first. This is the way of love and maturity. The strong are not held captive by the weak, but because of love they carefully exercise their Christ-won liberty. Again, knowledge puffs up, but love builds up. Knowledge can insist on all foods being clean, whereas love forgoes certain foods for the good of others.

> *"The strong are not held captive by the weak, but because of love they carefully exercise their Christ-won liberty."*

8:10 | *"For if someone with a weak conscience sees you, with all your knowledge, eating in an idol's temple, won't that person be emboldened to eat what is sacrificed to idols?"*

Idols' temples often had a dining room attached, in order to profitably dispose of all the food used in the offerings. It would have been normal and convenient for citizens of Corinth to eat in one of these. Whilst some of the mature believers knew that this food couldn't spoil their righteousness, some believers were struggling to free themselves from old thinking or patterns of behaviour. Pagan 'gods' needed to be appeased through food offerings, and followers of Christ needed to be free from this thinking. If recent converts saw mature Christ followers eating there, they may be encouraged to go back to old ways of living and relating to these idolatrous practices. Encouraging siblings to walk on the edge of a cliff path is neither wise nor loving.

8:11-12

> *"So this weak brother or sister, for whom Christ died, is destroyed by your knowledge. When you sin against them in this way and wound their weak conscience, you sin against Christ."*

Paul sums this section up with a stark warning: those who use knowledge without love can destroy the faith of others. Paul can't mean eternally destroyed, here; the sinful use of freedom can't remove other Christians from Christ's care (John 10v28). Rather, through foolish use of knowledge and liberty, they can pull down and wound the faith of weaker believers in the fellowship. As such, they not only sin against these brothers and sisters but also against Christ, who gave His life to give them life. We are saved into a family, and are responsible to one another. Knowledge is to be used with love, to express love, and to build up in love. Paul returns to the importance of love as the prime motive later in the letter.

> *"The way of love seeks to build one another up, rather than to insist on personal freedom."*

8:13

> *"Therefore, if what I eat causes my brother or sister to fall into sin, I will never eat meat again, so that I will not cause them to fall."*

Here, then, is Paul's summary statement about food sacrificed to idols: the way of love seeks to build one another up, rather than to insist on personal freedom. His readers are to limit their liberty if that helps a fellow believer with a weaker conscience. The important thing is to safeguard one another, doing everything possible to help their brothers and sisters grow and mature in faith. Yes, the Corinthian church is free to eat meat sacrificed to idols. Yet, they do better if they choose not to, if it causes another to weaken in their faith. It might seem here that 'sin' is a strong word. But if our actions cause weaker brothers and sisters to go back to their old allegiances, to these false gods, or to lose clarity on Christ's sufficiency, then sin is the appropriate word. "If anyone causes one of these little ones – those who believe in me – to stumble, it would be better for them to have a large millstone hung round their neck and to be drowned in the depths of the sea". (Matt 18v6)

CHAPTER 9

9:1 | *"Am I not free? Am I not an apostle? Have I not seen Jesus our Lord? Are you not the result of my work in the Lord?"*

The Corinthian church was started by Paul (Acts 18v1-17) so they would have known something of his story. He was an ambitious Pharisee who had zealously persecuted the followers of Jesus. He had travelled to Damascus to arrest believers, but encountered Christ en route (Acts 9v5). This was the defining moment of his life. God had chosen him as His instrument to carry the name of Jesus before the Gentiles, their kings, and the people of Israel (Acts 9v15). The prophets and teachers in Antioch confirmed this (Acts 13v2), as did the apostles in Jerusalem (15v24-29). His questions in this verse would all have been answered with a resounding "yes". He was the tentmaker who stayed with Aquila and Priscilla, who reasoned first in the synagogue and then in the house of Titius Justus, persuading both Jews and Greeks to follow Christ (Acts 18v7).

> *"a seal was used to denote ownership or as a guarantee of the authenticity and quality of a document or product."*

9:2 | *"Even though I may not be an apostle to others, surely I am to you! For you are the seal of my apostleship in the Lord."*

In these few words we see the high value Paul places on relationship and history. Paul recognises he may not be an apostle to other churches (presumably those he hadn't started or had any contact with), but he was to the Corinthian church. He laboured for 18 months, teaching them the Word of God despite opposition (Acts 18v6, 11). One night, in a vision, God spoke to Paul encouraging him to press on despite the persecution (Acts 18v9). So Paul reminds the Corinthians that they are the seal of his apostleship in the Lord. In those days, a seal was used to denote ownership or as a guarantee of the authenticity and quality of a document or product. Paul asserts that the Corinthians themselves are the proof that he is an apostle of Christ Jesus.

9:3

> *"This is my defence to those who sit in judgement on me."*

When it came to apostles, the believers in Corinth had strong preferences - if not prejudices - and there was much disagreement. Some followed Paul, some followed Apollos, some followed Cephas, and some even followed Christ! (1v12) Paul has already reminded them of the unity they have in Christ. Yet he also claims to be an apostle to them. For those who would still want to examine Paul's lifestyle and apostle credentials, he now lays out his defence. Church life is both glorious and messy, and always boils down to relationships. When it comes to the question of spiritual oversight, each of us want to relate to someone who is known to us, not just someone set over us in a leadership structure. Apostles do best when they appeal to their audience on the basis of an existing and ongoing relationship, rather than doctrine or tradition. Whilst it may feel clumsy to examine an apostle, much good can come from it if it is done in humility and good heartedness. Paul is willing to give a defence of himself to those who sit in judgement of him. The implication is that the hearers should be willing to listen with open hearts.

9:4

> *"Don't we have the right to food and drink?"*

Presumably some of the Corinthian factions (1v11) have criticised Paul for the financial support he is receiving from them. The church was in some sort of "present crisis" (7v26) which may have left some wondering why they were helping Paul. And yet he unapologetically argues he has the right to such support. After all, he has been commissioned by Jesus (9v1, Acts 9v5-6), and, like the Jewish Priesthood, he has the right to be supported by those he serves. While he was planting the church he made tents with Aquila and Priscilla (Acts 18v2) until Silas and Timothy came, who presumably were then able to support him. His primary goal was to be obedient and proclaim Christ (Gal 2v9) - it was never about getting free board and lodging. Whilst his calling gave him certain rights, he did not presume upon exercising them.

> *"Church life is both glorious and messy, and always boils down to relationships."*

9:5-6

> *"Don't we have the right to take a believing wife along with us, as do the other apostles and the Lord's brothers and Cephas? Or is it only I and Barnabas who lack the right to not work for a living?"*

Paul paints a picture of apostles travelling through Corinth with their wives, and both partners receiving hospitality. They are twice the burden, as husband and wife, and yet many of the Corinthians love following them. Paul is not saying this is wrong, but contrasting this practice with the criticism he has received. In the founding days of their church, Paul made tents alongside Priscilla and Aquila until he was supported by Silas and Timothy and could serve the church full-time. Like the other apostles, Paul had the right not to work, but he didn't want to be a burden. The reference to "the Lord's brothers" presumably includes James, a key leader of the Jerusalem church (Acts 15v13).

> ## *"This open-handed, common-sense generosity is the foundation of Paul's defence."*

9:7

> *"Who serves as a soldier at his own expense? Who plants a vineyard and does not eat its grapes? Who tends a flock and does not drink the milk?"*

These rhetorical questions all have the same answer: no-one. The soldier, farmer and shepherd all benefit from their employment; they have privileges linked to their profession. If it were not so, resentment would take root. If a soldier risks his life for his king, it is only right that he is equipped, fed and housed in his service. If even birds eat of the vine, how much more should those who tend the vineyard be refreshed from their labours? This open-handed, common-sense generosity is the foundation of Paul's defence to those who judge him for the material support he receives. The shepherd tends and cares for the flock in the open countryside, far from his home: who would resent him receiving nourishment from those he guards and leads?

9:8-9

"Do I say this merely on human authority? Doesn't the Law say the same thing? For it is written in the Law of Moses: "Do not muzzle an ox while it is treading out the grain." Is it about oxen that God is concerned?"

In arguing for the rights of an apostle, Paul appeals to Deuteronomy 25v4. Here, he finds an important truth buried in a directive on animal husbandry, and expands and applies this principle. In a similar way, Jesus argued that if God-fearing Jews are free to do the work of pulling an ox from a well on a sabbath, so He could do the work of healing on the Sabbath (Luke 14v3-6). God has a wider concern than for the beasts of burden. Just as an animal should not be frustrated by its hunger while it is serving its master, so should the apostle be fed by those he is serving. An ox will not eat all the grain, so a true apostle will not abuse his spiritual children. Sadly, Church history contains many stories of greed and abuse by those who should have been caring for and strengthening the flock. Nevertheless, despite human failings, the principle still stands.

> *"Jesus argued that if God-fearing Jews are free to do the work of pulling an ox from a well on a sabbath, so He could do the work of healing on the Sabbath"*

9:10

"Surely he says this for us, doesn't he? Yes, this was written for us, because whoever ploughs and threshes should be able to do so in the hope of sharing in the harvest."

Paul answers his own question, and quickly picks up another image to make his point. This picture, of farmhands sowing and reaping, would also have been very familiar to the Corinthians. The ploughman breaks up the ground, the seed grows, and months later the thresher works the gathered harvest. Both are to have a share in the crop, thereby fueling motivation of the workers. But it is also more than this: dignity and common sense are both served when this happens. It is easy to see the benefit of the workers having a share of the profits. God has written this principle into the fabric of life, and Paul draws this to their attention.

9:11

"If we have sown spiritual seed among you, is it too much if we reap a material harvest from you?"

Paul describes the Corinthians as a field that he has scattered gospel seed into, through hard work and personal cost. Surely he may reap a harvest from them? Spiritual seed can result in a material harvest. He argues "If others have this right of support from you, shouldn't we have it all the more?" These "others" are most likely the apostles referred to at the start of the letter (1v12): Apollos, Cephas, and so on. They have all sown spiritual seed into the Corinth - Paul does not deny this. And they reaped a material harvest, enough to support their spouses, who were travelling with them in their ministry (9v5). Paul is not against this practice, but reminds the Corinthians of the hospitality they extend to these visiting gospel servants. To those who criticise him, he simply asks he be judged in accordance with the practices of the other apostles who they hold in such high esteem.

9:12

"If others have this right of support from you, shouldn't we have it all the more? But we did not use this right. On the contrary, we put up with anything rather than hinder the gospel of Christ."

Having laid out the principle of apostles receiving material support from those they serve, Paul reminds them that he did not always use this right. This was Paul's way. Acts 20v33-35 records Paul's attitude as he says farewell to the Ephesian elders: "I have not coveted anyone's silver, gold or clothing. You yourselves know that these hands of mine have supplied my own needs and the needs of my companions." Paul wants to remove any and every obstacle for the gospel. If anyone should doubt his motive or accuse him of preaching for financial gain, then he would rather meet his own needs and put up with the resultant pressure. His record stands for itself. He is called to preach the good news of Jesus to the Gentiles, and he won't let anything hinder that calling. The comfort of coins never drew him from his calling. He had the right to ask for support from the Corinthians, because he planted the church, but he did not use it.

> *"The comfort of coins never drew him from his calling."*

9:13-14

"Don't you know that those who serve in the temple get their food from the temple, and that those who serve at the altar share in what is offered on the altar? In the same way, the Lord has commanded that those who preach the gospel should receive their living from the gospel."

Paul presumed that these Corinthian believers would be familiar with the Old Testament teaching on support of the priesthood. Leviticus 6v16 outlines the provision for Aaron and his sons to eat bread from the altar. Numbers 5v9 states that every sacred contribution brought to the priest to cover restitution of wrongs (and there would be a lot) should be theirs to enjoy. Deuteronomy 18v1 states that the "Lord's food offerings is their inheritance". So the ministers of God's grace have always been supported by those they serve. In the same way, those who preach the gospel should get their living by the gospel. This is applicable to local church leaders who proclaim Christ, as well as to those who travel amongst the churches strengthening them. Just as those who plough and thresh the fields hope to share in the harvest, so too do those who scatter and harvest gospel seed.

9:15

"But I have not used any of these rights. And I am not writing this in the hope that you will do such things for me, for I would rather die than allow anyone to deprive me of this boast."

As has already been noted, Paul's entrance into Corinthian life was as a tentmaker, working alongside Priscilla and Aquila. His financial strategy for church planting was clear: to not receive material support from those he was reaching. By so doing, he removed any accusations of personal financial gain or "conflicts of interest" - unlike the travelling speakers of Greek culture who expected to be paid for their oratory performances. In his following letter to them, he writes that he robbed other churches by accepting support from them in order to serve the Corinthians (2 Cor 11v8). The Philippians sent Epaphroditus to meet to his needs on their behalf; they entered into a giving and receiving partnership with him when no-one else did (Phil 2v25). Paul will not be robbed of this boast of joy. He has not and does not want their financial support; his life and track record demonstrate that.

"Just as those who plough and thresh the fields hope to share in the harvest, so too do those who scatter and harvest gospel seed."

9:16

"For when I preach the gospel, I cannot boast, since I am compelled to preach. Woe to me if I do not preach the gospel!"

Despite Paul's success in soul-winning and church-planting, he has nothing to boast about. He doesn't really have a choice in the matter, for he is living with a deep compulsion that he can't or won't suppress. He regards this task as "a necessity laid upon me" (ESV). It is something that gives him joy, a sense of fulfilment and a motivation that money couldn't buy. If Paul did not preach 'Christ risen from the dead', it would bring a great sadness upon him. His conviction and sense of calling are strong. His motive for Gospel proclamation is beyond question. He has foregone material support, which he has a right to, in order to discharge his duty without any hint of personal financial gain. He is compelled to preach Christ for the glory of God and the benefit of others.

> *"Rendering the service voluntarily is what reaps the reward and brings benefit to the steward."*

9:17

"If I preach voluntarily, I have a reward; if not voluntarily, I am simply discharging the trust committed to me."

The ESV talks of being entrusted with 'stewardship', the same word used for the manager of a household. Paul has been entrusted with the responsibility of proclaiming the gospel, and he must do this. He is obliged to discharge his duties regardless of personal outcomes or his own preferences. It is interesting that he refers to doing so 'voluntarily' or 'not voluntarily'. This is unlikely to mean preaching under a form of duress. Most likely he is making the point that a wise steward must discharge the duties entrusted to him regardless of his feelings or preferences. Being a good steward is what counts. It is worth noting that rendering the service voluntarily is what reaps the reward and brings benefit to the steward. This paints a vivid picture of how Paul views himself: the faithful Gospel steward proclaiming Christ in season and out of season (2 Tim 4v2).

9:18

> *"What then is my reward? Just this: that in preaching the gospel I may offer it free of charge, and so not make full use of my rights as a preacher of the gospel."*

Most of us assume that exercising our rights will reap rewards. Not so for Paul. His reward is to not make use of his rights. This is unusual, but compelling. He knows what he is about: he's a gospel herald. Discharging this duty as best he can is what floats his boat. Yes, he had the right to support during his stay with the Corinthians, yet he chose not to receive it. His new teaching was solely for their good, not for his benefit. He wants to proclaim the gospel without any burden to the hearer. Just as Christ bore the cost to proclaim good news, so Paul follows suit. He has removed another stumbling block to his listeners and critics; his motive is above reproach. He offers the gospel free of charge. This approach sets him apart from the itinerant orators of his day, who would rely on the donations of their listeners.

> *"Rather than exercising his rights, he yields them; rather than elevating himself he humbles himself."*

9:19

> *"Though I am free and belong to no one, I have made myself a slave to everyone, to win as many as possible."*

Paul uses evocative language to express his compulsion to proclaim Christ. To those who have criticised him he now turns his argument to unexpected depths. While other apostles exercise their rights for financial support, Paul not only refuses to do that but instead considers himself a "slave". Rather than exercising his rights, he yields them; rather than elevating himself he humbles himself. He uses his freedom in Christ to make himself a slave to everyone. Why? In order to win as many as possible to Christ. He offers his service free of charge; the true cost is paid by the Father and Son. The freed man is enslaved by love, and this is why he proclaims hope to lost souls. Paul's life is now motivated and defined by service to all who will listen, in order to win as many as possible.

9:20 *"To the Jews I became like a Jew, to win the Jews. To those under the law I became like one under the law (though I myself am not under the law), so as to win those under the law."*

Paul was willing to do whatever it took to proclaim Christ to lost people. If that meant forsaking his rights as an apostle, so be it. If that meant living like a Jew in order to reach Jews, so be it. This explains why he circumcised Timothy (Acts 16v3), and also paid for the purification costs of four brothers who had made vows in Jerusalem. He was willing and prepared to live under Jewish cultural and religious frameworks if that gained him a hearing. Paul's identity was secure: he was an apostle of Christ Jesus, by the will of God; he was called to preach to the Gentiles (1 Cor 1v1, Gal 2v9, Rom 15v16). And he still longed to proclaim Christ to his Jewish brothers (Rom 11v31).

9:21 *"To those not having the law I became like one not having the law (though I am not free from God's law but am under Christ's law), so as to win those not having the law."*

Paul, like the apostle Peter in Acts 10, was propelled to cross religious divides despite everything in his cultural background screaming at him not to. Peter's vision was repeated three times, presumably to press home the conviction and to cut through his prejudice (Acts 10v9-17). Peter was obedient, and as a result Cornelius, his relatives and his close friends all responded to the gospel (Acts 10v23-48). Paul also overcame his Pharisaical prejudices and was willing to live as if he didn't have the law in order to win non-Jews. The law of Christ is probably best understood to include Christ's teaching in his earthly ministry - which built on and fulfilled the moral codes of Mosaic Law - as well as what we now have in the New Testament, which is the apostle's application of Christ's teaching.

> *"The law of Christ is probably best understood to include Christ's teaching in his earthly ministry."*

9:22

> *"To the weak I became weak, to win the weak. I have become all things to all people so that by all possible means I might save some."*

Paul has already encouraged the Corinthians to accommodate believers with a weak conscience (8 v9-13). Now he turns that same thinking to winning weak unbelievers. It is not clear in what way they were "weak". The point is that mature believers are to come alongside 'weak unbelievers' in humility and meekness. The goal is the salvation of the unbeliever, and that requires Christ-like condescension. Believers are to voluntarily embrace equality with those who are weaker in order that they may hear the gospel with dignity. Or, to put it another way, believers are to voluntarily put aside their own position and assume equality with someone who is regarded as socially inferior. Grace starts by relating downwards. Paul urges the Corinthians to embrace their freedom to be all things to all people, so that by all possible means they might save some.

9:23

> *"I do all this for the sake of the gospel, that I may share in its blessings."*

Whilst Paul did not use his right of support from the churches he planted (v12), he does want to share in the blessings of the gospel. He is certain that as he discharges his gospel duty, so he shares in its blessing. As he blesses, so is he blessed. It is to his advantage, for he has in mind a prize that surpasses all (v24-27). He knows that the Lord of the harvest, the captain of the army (v7), the owner of the sheep, will amply reward those who faithfully serve his purposes. God is able and willing to bless His faithful stewards. The heavenly Master has inexhaustible blessings to share. Paul proclaims Christ with an eye on the blessing of heralding the gospel.

"Grace starts by relating downwards."

9:24

"Do you not know that in a race all the runners run, but only one gets the prize? Run in such a way as to get the prize."

Paul turns now to an athletic metaphor, which would have been easy for the Corinthians to connect with as their city hosted the Isthmian games - an event second only to the Olympics. Paul draws on the single-minded dedication required by the athletes taking part. This imagery helps to describe his rigor and focus in pursuing the call of God on his life. He is running to win. He is not interested in being someone who 'also ran' in the things of God. It's not that he wanted to beat everyone. Rather, he knew and loved the One who gave the prizes. So he will spend himself and "press on toward the goal for the prize of the upward call of God in Christ Jesus" (Phi 3v14). The same metaphor recurs elsewhere. The writer to the Hebrews says "let us also lay aside every weight and sin which clings so closely, and let us run with endurance the race that is set before us" (Heb 12v1). We, too, are to run in such a way as to get the prize.

> *"It's not that he wanted to beat everyone. Rather, he knew and loved the One who gave the prizes."*

9:25

"Everyone who competes in the games goes into strict training. They do it to get a crown that will not last, but we do it to get a crown that will last forever."

A champion crown at the Isthmian games was a wreath, probably made from pine leaves, that would inevitably perish. What was important wasn't the value of the wreath in itself, but the great honoured it bestowed. Competitors undertook rigorous training in order to win the right to wear it. Self-control, dedication and pain are the athlete's friends of choice in their preparation. How much more, then, argues Paul, should those who follow Christ go into strict training to receive a crown that is imperishable? The great surprise is that the Corinthians are the crown Paul has in mind! They are the imperishable wreath; they are his victor's crown! Apostles go into strict training to win congregations for Christ. The Corinthians are the evidence of Paul's focused labour and fruitfulness.

9:26-27

"Therefore I do not run like someone running aimlessly; I do not fight like a boxer beating the air. No, I strike a blow to my body and make it my slave so that after I have preached to others, I myself will not be disqualified for the prize."

The Isthmian games included sports like wrestling, boxing, and Greek martial arts (Pankration). Paul's readers would have been familiar with these activities, the training required for them, and the stakes involved in such physical contact! Paul ran his race to win the prize; he's not running aimlessly. He is fighting his fight to deliver a knockout punch. He wants to find his mark and deliver a decisive blow. He knows the prize and is acting accordingly; the prize is shaping his performance. Using this athletic metaphor, Paul is expressing his single-mindedness in achieving his goal: to bring as many people to faith in Jesus Christ as he is able. He is focussed, intentional, and undivided. His eye is on the prize.

CHAPTER 10

10:1

"For I do not want you to be ignorant of the fact, brothers and sisters, that our ancestors were all under the cloud and that they all passed through the sea."

Paul brings his readers' thoughts to the days when God took His people out of slavery in Egypt. Their spiritual ancestors were led by a tangible, visible cloud that led and protected them through a wilderness, and to and through the Red Sea. God hears the cry of his people, but demands an active faith. Exodus 13v17-14v31 records that the Lord went before His people in a pillar of cloud by day and fire by night. This was the beginning of a journey of testing, but some disqualified themselves from receiving their prize. Paul reminds the Corinthian believers, both Jews and Gentiles, that they are caught up in this bigger story. The lessons of the exodus will serve this church well.

> *"Participating in the miraculous events (following the pillar of cloud, and passing through the sea) 'joined' them to the promise-holder, Moses."*

10:2

"They were all baptised into Moses in the cloud and in the sea."

Baptism is an outward demonstration of an internal spiritual reality. Paul sees this huge event in Israel's history, the exodus, as the defining moment that demonstrates that a transition has taken place. These people were called out of slavery to a foreign king and brought under God's care through Moses. Once they were a despised people, working as slaves to Pharaoh. But now they are the called-out people of God, a holy nation. The pillar of cloud and parting of the sea were outward demonstrations of God choosing and leading them into freedom. Moses was the promise-holder; he was commissioned by God himself to lead His people to freedom in the promised homeland. Participating in the miraculous events (following the pillar of cloud, and passing through the sea) 'joined' them to the promise-holder, Moses. This was a rite of passage identifying them as recipients of the promises given to Moses; in a sense, they were 'baptised' into Moses. He became their federal head and they became part of the Kingdom he represented: God's.

10:3-4

"They all ate the same spiritual food and drank the same spiritual drink; for they drank from the spiritual rock that accompanied them, and that rock was Christ."

During Israel's desert wanderings, God provided physical sustenance: manna, quail, and water from the rock at Horeb (Exo 16, 17v1-7). Paul is saying that these physical, outward events were symbolic of a spiritual reality. In some real but mystical way, the pre-incarnate Christ was travelling with them. He fully identified with them, and was active in sustaining and refreshing them. He was ever present with God's people. During his incarnate ministry, Christ claimed to be the true bread of life who comes down from heaven (John 6v35) and to be the source of living water (John 4v10). Christ is the spiritual rock they drank from; he was sustaining his people. King David describes God as his rock, fortress, deliverer, and place of refuge (Psa 18v2). These are the qualities of Christ the spiritual rock, too.

10:5

"Nevertheless, God was not pleased with most of them; their bodies were scattered in the wilderness."

Here, then, is the shock: the beloved fell short and were judged. Paul will go on to give the reasons for their failing, but for now we should stop and consider this verse. Despite them being baptised into Moses, despite having the pillar of cloud by day and fire by night, despite passing through a sea, despite receiving manna, quail and water from the rock at Horeb, despite Christ accompanying them, despite all this, their actions were such that God was not pleased with most of them. They had seen genuine miracles, yet few responded with saving faith. They heard God's voice, yet they rebelled. They had his presence in a cloud, yet they continued to lack faith in the wilderness. God swore that the disobedient would not enter his rest. They tested God ten times and did not obey His voice, and so God declared that they would not see the land he swore to give them (Num 14v22-23). This cautionary lesson is repeated by the writer to the Hebrews: "So we see that they were not able to enter because of unbelief" (Heb 3v16-19).

> *"In some real but mystical way, the pre-incarnate Christ was travelling with them."*

10:6

"Now these things occurred as examples to keep us from setting our hearts on evil things as they did."

Paul wants the Corinthians to be fully aware of the scriptures' examples and warnings, "For whatever was written in former days was written for our instruction, that through endurance and the encouragement of the Scriptures we might have hope" (Rom 15v4). These events of salvation and rebellion have been recorded to instruct us. They are examples of how not to respond to God's grace: we should not presume upon unending favour, not be casual about the holiness of God, not long after and be engrossed by evil things. God was willing to let Israel die in the wilderness so that we might be be aware of His character. Yes, He is for us, and yes, He wants to keep our hearts from desiring evil. But these tragic events, immortalised in Israel's history, were to act as a very public warning.

> *"These tragic events, immortalised in Israel's history, were to act as a very public warning."*

10:7

"Do not be idolaters, as some of them were; as it is written: "'The people sat down to eat and drink and got up to indulge in revelry.'"

Paul goes on to catalogue some of the things their forefathers did that displeased God. Firstly, they were idolaters. While Moses was meeting with God on Mount Sinai, the people got tired of waiting and demanded from Aaron "Come, makes us gods who will go before us". Exodus 32 records how Aaron did what they asked: using the gold they donated, he cast an idol in the image of a calf. Moses' brother had his chance to shine, but he led God's people in a festival of burnt offerings and revelry (Ex 32v5-6). Paul warns the Corinthians to learn from this lesson: delays expose what is in our hearts. Aaron should have told the people to trust in God and wait for his brother. Instead, their impatience and arrogance was exposed. They became idolaters, settling for a man- made shadow; this aroused the anger and judgement of the supreme reality. It is possible for God's people to so arouse His anger that He threatens to destroy them (Ex 32v10).

10:8

"We should not commit sexual immorality, as some of them did—and in one day twenty-three thousand of them died."

Numbers 25v1 records that "While Israel was staying in Shittim, the men began to indulge in sexual immorality with Moabite women who invited them to the sacrifices to their gods." So begins another stark lesson from the history of God's people. Their sexual immorality began a chain of events that unleashed the Lord's anger against them. God initiated a plague that killed 2,400 of his people. It only relented when a spear was driven through a flagrantly rebellious man and his Midianite wife. These verses can easily offend our sensibilities, surely there must have be an alternative to the death penalty? Why weren't they given a final warning, another opportunity to repent? But we need to recognise the sinfulness of sin and trust the holiness of God. Paul urges the Corinthians to master their sexual appetites and to meet these desires within the context of their marriages.

> *"The Corinthians needed to learn the lessons from history and trust in Christ's ongoing leadership and sufficiency."*

10:9

"We should not test Christ, as some of them did—and were killed by snakes."

Numbers 21v5 describes how the Israelites grumbled against God about food, water and his guidance. He responded by sending venomous serpents among them, which bit the people, many of whom died. Thankfully, the people quickly came to their senses and repented, asking Moses to pray for them. God then told him to make a bronze serpent, and to it up high so that "whoever has been bitten may look to it and be saved". Paul previously stated that Christ was with his people in the desert wandering (v4); therefore, the lesson is not to test Christ. The Corinthians needed to learn the lessons from history and trust in Christ's ongoing leadership and sufficiency. Jesus referred to this bronze serpent as a foreshadow of himself (John 3:14). Judgement is indeed coming, but so too is God's Saviour who gives eternal life. Looking to the serpent to be healed prefigures looking in faith to Christ.

10:10

"And do not grumble, as some of them did—and were killed by the destroying angel."

The Israelites were grumblers on a mission. They had passed through the Red Sea, eaten manna from heaven, drunk water from the rock - they were even accompanied by the pre-incarnate Christ. And yet they grumbled to Moses and against God. This was an ongoing trend. Numbers 14 records that when the spies returned and gave their report of Canaan, the people quickly forgot Joshua and Caleb's account. They listened to the wrong people, forgot their recent history, and grumbled against their leaders and God. As a result, some were then destroyed by the consuming angel. Here, then, is the warning: we are not to assume the compassion, mercy and love of God trumps His holiness, jealousy or justice. He is concerned with our hearts more than with our comfort. The destroying angel is not mentioned in Numbers, but there is a reference to the destroyer in Exodus 12v23 at the Passover (see also Hebrews 11v28).

10:11

"These things happened to them as examples and were written down as warnings for us, on whom the culmination of the ages has come."

You could argue that v1-5 are examples of God's provision and care whilst v7-10 warn the Corinthians not to respond as their forefathers did. Those of us who are living in the days after Christ's resurrection can enjoy the benefit of these historical examples and warnings, but only if we heed them. Scripture is clearly more than just a written history documenting what happened. It is also the Spirit's 'work of provision' for us who believe. It reveals God's faithful provision, and his people's hard hearts. As Paul says, scripture is important for our everyday lives as a means of encouragement and admonishment: "All Scripture is God breathed and is useful for teaching, rebuking, correcting and training in righteousness, so that the man of God may be thoroughly equipped for every good work" (2 Tim 3v16).

> *"We are not to assume the compassion, mercy and love of God trumps His holiness, jealousy or justice."*

10:12 | *"So, if you think you are standing firm, be careful that you don't fall!"*

Paul is most likely referring to the Corinthians, who through exercising their freedom in Christ are exposing themselves and others to stumbling (8v9). As the proverb wisely warns, "pride goes before destruction, and a haughty spirit before a fall" (Pro 16v18). Paul cautions these beloved believers to guard against complacency. Many gave heartfelt thanks to God as they left Egypt, but became grumblers in the desert. Like them, we all are capable of both faithful obedience and wilful rebellion - sometimes in the same moment. Those who think they are standing firm "should be sober minded and set their hope fully on the grace that will be revealed in Christ Jesus" (1 Pet 1v13). Complacency will not lead to holiness. We are to be on our guard, watching our life and doctrine closely (1 Tim 4v16).

10:13 | *"No temptation has overtaken you except what is common to mankind. And God is faithful; he will not let you be tempted beyond what you can bear. But when you are tempted, he will also provide a way out so that you can endure it."*

The Christian who is standing firm still has to face the same temptations that are common to all: unbelief, greed, lust, envy, pride, laziness, idolatry, anger towards the innocent. And so Paul directs their attention to the character of their God: He is faithful and compassionate. The heavenly Father uses the pressure of living in a broken world to bring us into maturity. But He does not allow us to be tested to destruction; there is always a way out. Temptation always comes with a way of escape. Endurance can bring maturity. As one commentator has written: "Even when Christians face morally confusing situations, they should never think that they have no options other than sinful ones. There will always be a morally right solution that does not require disobedience to God's moral laws" (ESV Study bible).

> *"Many gave heartfelt thanks to God as they left Egypt, but became grumblers in the desert."*

10:14 | *"Therefore, my dear friends, flee from idolatry."*

Paul's summary is simple: the people are to "flee from idolatry". They shouldn't try to resist or manage it, they should simply run away from anything that might capture or engross their hearts. They are to flee anything that might replace God as their primary source of identity, purpose, well being or hope. While other religions permitted and depended upon the worship of their idols, Paul urges the Corinthians not to follow suit. Yes, they can eat meat sacrificed to idols, but they should never worship one. Idolatry is a peril, a grave danger to be avoided (v7). Idolatry was a real and everyday part of Corinthian life, a familiar activity that most of Paul's readers likely used to partake in. But now they have turned to Christ; they have given him their allegiance. As such, they are to be distinctive, to be set apart for their jealous God (Exo 20v5, 34v4).

> *"They are to flee anything that might replace God as their primary source of identity, purpose, well being or hope."*

10:15-16 | *"I speak to sensible people; judge for yourselves what I say. Is not the cup of thanksgiving for which we give thanks a participation in the blood of Christ? And is not the bread that we break a participation in the body of Christ?"*

Paul is building a reasoned argument for reasonable people: idolatry arouses the Lord's jealousy (v22). He bases his argument on the sacrament of communion (Matt 26v26-28). When the people drink from that cup and break that bread, they are identifying with Christ and trusting in His sufficiency. Christ made exclusive claims, such as being the only way to the Father, and therefore demands a wholehearted response. No groom is indifferent about his fiancee's fidelity. Just as a groom is jealous for his bride, so Christ is jealous for us. Our participation in communion is a sign of our ongoing faith in and faithfulness to Christ. To participate with thanksgiving means to joyfully share fellowship with, and align yourself to, Christ's cause. This being the case, it makes no sense to participate in idol feasts which are in opposition to Christ.

10:17

> *"Because there is one loaf, we, who are many, are one body, for we all share the one loaf."*

Paul continues his line of thought using the symbolism of the Lord's Supper. When Jesus broke the bread he said "this is my body"; his disciples were unified by the act of eating from the one loaf. This sacrament - partaking in the bread and wine - was given as a means of demonstrating unity and equality. Together, believers in Christ share one loaf regardless of background or social standing. All were invited; all were included. There were no special portions or dietary requirements. Communion is as much an expression of unity as it is about identity and spiritual sustenance. The Corinthians are to "feast" on Christ as one body; they gather around His table and their hearts are gladdened by His wine. Christ has united them.

> *"Communion is as much an expression of unity as it is about identity and spiritual sustenance."*

10:18

> *"Consider the people of Israel: Do not those who eat the sacrifices participate in the altar?"*

Paul most likely has in mind here the table of showbread in the tabernacle. It stood within the Holy Place, holding twelve loaves of bread, which were always kept fresh (Ex 25v30). Only priests could eat the bread, but it symbolised God's desire to have fellowship and communion with His people. If a priest ever had doubt about God's intent towards humankind, he was reminded of God's generosity by this invitation to share a meal with Him. It was an expression of friendship that was always in place, always available. This is a fitting parallel for Paul's discussion about idol feasts and the Lord's Supper. Every Sabbath the Priests would participate in fellowship with God by eating the showbread. Equally, Paul could be referring to the animals sacrificed on the bronze altar as the first steps for approaching a holy God. Again, the priests were entitled to eat a portion of the sacrificed meat.

10:19-20

"Do I mean then that food sacrificed to an idol is anything, or that an idol is anything? No, but the sacrifices of pagans are offered to demons, not to God, and I do not want you to be participants with demons."

Isaiah records that idols are made of wood, part of this was used to kindle a fire to bake bread, and another piece was used to make an object of worship (Isa 44 v15-17). In itself, an idol and the sacrifice offered to it can be thought of as nothing. However, demons are behind the deception. The demonic realm is real and active. Demons are agents of the dominion of darkness. They are created beings, angels who rebelled against God, enemies of God and His people. They are many and powerful. And their rebellion has a ringleader: Satan. Satan tried to get God to bow down and worship him (Matt 8v9-10), so his demons try to do the same to those made in God's image. Jesus refused, and so must the Corinthians. Idols are both nothing and something. They are merely works of craftsmen, but also the tools of demons, used to entrap and destroy.

10:21

"You cannot drink the cup of the Lord and the cup of demons too; you cannot have a part in both the Lord's table and the table of demons."

Paul uses the evocative image of the two tables at which the Corinthians can eat and have fellowship. One is the Lord's table; the other is a table of demons. Either they drink from His cup of life, or from a cup of destruction. Either they feast on Him as the bread of life, or they eat poison served at the table of darkness. They are mutually exclusive: you can't have a seat at both tables. One table is spiritual life and fellowship with Christ; the other is spiritual death and servitude to demons. Either they are seated with Christ in heavenly realms, or they cower for scraps at the table of demons.

Note: Eating food sacrificed to idols is different to eating at the table of demons (to fellowship with, or be sustained by, the demonic). The Corinthians are free to eat food that has been sacrificed to an idol if they do so in faith, weren't involved the worship itself, and it doesn't cause a weaker believer to stumble. Food does not make them further from God when eaten with faith in Christ (8v8).

> *"Satan tried to get God to bow down and worship him (Matt 8v9-10), so his demons try to do the same to those made in God's image."*

10:22 | *"Are we trying to arouse the Lord's jealousy? Are we stronger than he?"*

The God of the bible is a jealous God: "They have made me jealous with what is no god; they have provoked me to anger with their idols" (Deu 32v21); "You shall not bow down to carved images or serve them, for I the Lord your God am a jealous God" (Exo 20v5). Jealousy is not the sinful emotion of envy; rather, it is the appropriate response of a holy God. God is the Creator, the Sustainer and the Truth. He is zealous for His name, and well able to defend it. To arouse His jealousy, to intentionally provoke it, is foolish. His wrath may only last for a moment, but it is all consuming. Only fools willingly provoke a husband's jealousy: "jealousy makes a man furious, and he will not spare when he takes revenge" (Pro 9v34). Paul warns the Corinthians against arousing such jealousy.

10:23 | *"'I have the right to do anything,' you say—but not everything is beneficial. 'I have the right to do anything'—but not everything is constructive."*

Here Paul repeats the refrain of 6v12, presumably because it was a popular phrase in the Corinthian church. That everything was lawful and permissible must have been a hugely difficult idea to those with a Jewish heritage. God's people now had freedom to pursue all manner of activities and choices. But those choices are to be bound and governed by principles of love and wisdom. The people are to act in a way that will not inhibit the advance of the gospel (9v12, 22). They are not to exercise their freedom in a way that becomes a stumbling block to weaker brothers or to unbelievers (8v9, 10v27-28). Liberty is to function for the good of a community; it is to bless rather than harm, it is to be considerate rather than assertive.

> *"To arouse His jealousy, to intentionally provoke it, is foolish."*

10:24

"No one should seek their own good, but the good of others."

Paul encourages the Corinthians to put the good of others first. Freedom, with love, self-regulates. Liberty, with love, chooses restriction "Those who are strong have an obligation to bear with the failings of the weak, and not to please ourselves" (Rom 15v1). For those who follow Christ, there are no exceptions. No Christ follower should use their freedom solely for their own good. The servant must follow his master, and their master took the nature of a bondservant (Phi 2v7). Those who follow Jesus are to use their freedom wisely, in a way that strengthens the wider body of believers (16-17). While everything is permissible, Christians are to choose that which is beneficial, constructive, and good for others. The freedom given by Christ is to lead us to seek the good of others; we are to make choices that put the good of others first.

> *"Freedom, with love, self-regulates. Liberty, with love, chooses restriction."*

10:25-26

"Eat anything sold in the meat market without raising questions of conscience, for, 'The earth is the Lord's, and everything in it.'"

Paul releases the Corinthians to purchase and consume anything sold at the meat market. Much of this meat would have come from the sacrifices at the various pagan temples. Paul urges them to make no distinction; they are to be confident that nothing can make them 'unclean'. Everything belongs to God, and He has given it to them for their good. This was radical thinking. Creation has been redeemed, and God's people are set apart through faith in Christ so now everything is permissible to eat. Consciences, once governed by restrictions, must now be tenderly re-educated and brought into line with the new covenant. Those accustomed to idols need to come into the liberty won for them by Christ, "through whom all things came and through whom we live" (8v6).

10:27

"If an unbeliever invites you to a meal and you want to go, eat whatever is put before you without raising questions of conscience."

Paul moves to an example, of being invited to an unbeliever's house for a meal. The assumption is that the Corinthian believers are not a 'holy huddle' but part of - and liked by! - the communities around them. This in itself is a challenge to us. Once such an invitation is received, and if the believer wants to go, they are free to attend and to eat whatever is put before them. Long gone are the restrictions on meat and eating with Gentiles in Peter's vision of Acts 10v12-14 . Yet it was hard for the Jewish believers to overcome this thinking. Even the apostles Peter and Barnabas stopped eating with Gentiles, and had to be rebuked by Paul (Gal 2v11-13). This mistake is not to be repeated by the Corinthians.

> *"Paul urges the strong believer to be careful about exercising their freedom."*

10:28

"But if someone says to you, 'This has been offered in sacrifice,' then do not eat it, both for the sake of the one who told you and for the sake of conscience."

Paul pictures the scenario of being invited for a meal and the host makes a deliberate point to mention that the food was offered in a pagan ritual. Presumably they did so because they are a believer with a weak conscience, or an unbeliever who wants to test their guest, or a concerned unbeliever who, in friendship, is letting their Christian friend know 'just in case'.

Given the context, it is most likely the host is a believer with a weak conscience (8v10). Paul urges the strong believer to be careful about exercising their freedom. He writes that if eating meat causes a brother to fall, he would rather never eat meat again (8v13). But for whichever reason the statement is made, Paul urges the believer not to eat, to honour the host's conscience.

10:29-30

"I am referring to the other person's conscience, not yours. For why is my freedom being judged by another's conscience? If I take part in the meal with thankfulness, why am I denounced because of something I thank God for?"

Another translation of the bible renders this line as: "Why should my liberty be determined by someone else's conscience?" (ESV). Once again, Paul reminds the Corinthians that he, like them, is at liberty to take part in any meal if he does so with faith, a clear conscience, and thankfulness to God. Like him, they are free to do this. Yes, out of love and concern for a weaker believer, they may choose to abstain. But Paul's conscience remains clear: to eat is not wrong. In essence, he is contending for gospel advance by all means, even embracing restrictions. He even wants to avoid others unnecessarily judging his clear conscience. So, even when he can eat with thankfulness, he would prefer to abstain if it means others aren't provoked to judge him.

10:31

"So whether you eat or drink or whatever you do, do it all for the glory of God."

Everything is permissible, and everyone should seek the good of others. Anything and everything can be eaten with thankfulness and a clear conscience, and this can be done in such a way that it brings brings glory, honour and esteem to God. Christ's followers can worship as they eat, enjoying the freedom of an unrestricted menu. This should be done for the good of others; this should be a liberty that blesses not wounds. Love transcends appetites and looks to strengthen the weak for the glory of God. The weak brother (8v10) is to be encouraged through the mature believer's abstention, for the glory of God. The unbelieving host is to be honoured without raising questions of conscience, for the glory of God. Meat bought in the market is to be enjoyed, for the glory of God. In fact, whatever they do, the Corinthians' motive and goal must be to bring glory, honour and thanksgiving to God.

> *"Love transcends appetites and looks to strengthen the weak for the glory of God."*

10:32 | *"Do not cause anyone to stumble, whether Jews, Greeks or the church of God-"*

Paul encourages these believers to use their freedom for the common good of Jews, Greeks, and the church alike. Grace should be expressed to all. Both those far from Christ and those hidden in Christ are to be blessed by His hard-won freedom. For Paul, to have no regard as to how our choices affect others is unthinkable. Christians must "decide never to put a stumbling block or hindrance in the way of a brother" (Rom 14v13). We are our brother's keeper. Christ alone is to be the stumbling block and rock of offence (Isa 8v14, Rom 9v33), not the use of our freedom in Him.

10:33 | *"even as I try to please everyone in every way. For I am not seeking my own good but the good of many, so that they may be saved."*

Here we see Paul the people-pleaser. While this may seem contrary to his reprimands of 5v2 and 6v7, it is nonetheless true. His motive is not to be the most popular apostle or visiting speaker, but that many would be saved. He uses his freedom "to become all things to all men so that by all possible means I might save some" (9v22). He is not seeking his own advantage, rather that the grace and peace from God the Father and the Lord Jesus Christ would come to many (1v3). The Corinthians have been enriched in every way because of his testimony about Christ (1v5). Paul, the people-pleaser, wants to bring the message of the cross - which is foolishness to those who are perishing - to everybody in every way, because it is the power of God for salvation (1v18). Paul can only speak; ultimately, it is God who saves.

> *"His motive is not to be the most popular apostle or visiting speaker, but that many would be saved."*

CHAPTER 11

11:1 | *"Follow my example, as I follow the example of Christ."*

Paul endeavoured to give glory to God in whatever he did. He sought not to let his freedom cause others to stumble, but to please everybody in every way in order that they may be saved. Paul calls the Corinthians to follow his example, as he follows Christ's. Christ did not seek his own glory but chose instead to reveal the Father's. Christ was a friend of gluttons, drunkards, tax collectors and sinners, but was a stumbling block to the religious (Luke 7v34). Jesus did all this to win the people's hearts, so that they may believe in Him and be saved. Paul was following Christ's example: Christ's freedom and liberty was used for the benefit and well being of others; Christ's freedom was used to save others. Paul follows suit, and asks the church in Corinth to do likewise.

> *"Presumably each apostle had a certain emphasis, and if these differences were mishandled it caused unintended divisions."*

11:2 | *"I praise you for remembering me in everything and for holding to the traditions just as I passed them on to you."*

Just as the Thessalonians remember Paul kindly, and longed to see him again (1 Thess 3v6), so do the Corinthians. Paul, their father in Christ (4v15), commends them for remembering him and his teachings. It seems that the apostles' teaching was circulating amongst the churches. Presumably each apostle had a certain emphasis, and if these differences were mishandled it caused unintended divisions (1v12). Paul commends the Corinthians for maintaining the traditions he delivered to them. Paul's message and preaching were not with wise and persuasive words, but with a demonstration of the Spirit's power (2v4), which no doubt made his teaching memorable and authoritative. Paul planned to send Timothy to visit them, to help the Corinthians to continue imitating his ways in Christ and to teach in every church (4v17).

11:3

"But I want you to realise that the head of every man is Christ, and the head of the woman is man, and the head of Christ is God."

The term head can be understood to mean "to have authority over"; as Paul writes elsewhere, Christ is the head of the church (Eph 1v22). God the Son is equal in deity with God the Father, yet He willingly chooses to do the Father's will (John 7v16, Luke 22v42). Just as there is equality and headship in the Godhead, so is there equality and headship in marriage. The wife is equal in personhood, value and honour to her husband, yet she is to willingly choose to do his will. The husband is the head of his wife, yet he must willing choose to do the will of Christ. Christ is the head of the husband, yet he willingly chooses to do the will of God the Father. The Father's will is good and loving it cascades down to bless His Son, and husbands, and wives. As Christ works for the wellbeing of the church, so husbands are to work for the wellbeing of their wives. This flow of headship and willing submission demands trust and a conviction that marriage echoes Christ's relationship to His church (Eph 5v22).

11:4

"Every man who prays or prophesies with his head covered dishonors his head."

Trying to make sense of this verse requires some understanding of the cultural practices of the day. That is never as precise as we might hope, but here's my best shot. It was common during acts of pagan worship for men to pull a fold of their robe up over their head when praying to their idol. It was a way of showing reverence and submission, much like a curtsey or a bow when first greeting a British monarch. Most likely, the Corinthian men were using this same pagan means of expressing reverence: Paul considers this inappropriate and absurd. Whatever the exact motives were, it is Paul's view that men covering their heads to pray or prophesy during meetings brought dishonour and discredit to Christ. Whilst we now have great freedom from ritual and form, how something is done remains important. We must worship in a way that isn't a stumbling block to unbelievers. Meat offered to idols can be eaten so long as unbelievers or immature believers are not confused or offended. Men are to pray and prophesy during church meetings in a way that acknowledges the cultural sensitivities of onlookers.

> *"This flow of headship and willing submission demands trust and a conviction that marriage echoes Christ's relationship to His church."*

11:5

"But every woman who prays or prophesies with her head uncovered dishonours her head—it is the same as having her head shaved."

Corinthian culture was based on honour and shame; the culture of the contemporary West is motivated by law and guilt. This is why Paul speaks about the shame brought to Christ when men pray and prophesy in a way that reflects pagan practices. Corinthian culture was complex in that it valued both modesty and promiscuity. Corinthian men wanted their wives to be faithful, but would use prostitutes. Paul wanted life to be different for the church, so he gives instructions to the women and wives (the ESV specifies "wife"). Wives were expected to cover their heads, either as a sign of their modesty or as a commitment to their marriage. Not to do so would bring shame on their community and on her husband (much like in conservative Muslim countries today). A parallel for us might be for a married woman to deliberately and demonstrably take off her wedding ring just before prophesying in church. That would be awkward for all - especially her husband.

> *"Wives were expected to cover their heads, either as a sign of their modesty or as a commitment to their marriage."*

11:6

"For if a woman does not cover her head, she might as well have her hair cut off; but if it is a disgrace for a woman to have her hair cut off or her head shaved, then she should cover her head."

Paul is not making a case for punishment but for a deterrent: he is seeking to safeguard the honour of the gospel. For whatever reason, it was shameful for a woman to speak with her hair uncovered. As such, with the intention that people would be saved (10v33), women (or wives) should try to please all people everywhere by acknowledging local culture and use their freedom wisely. Paul wants the church to be the place where Christ is worshipped, rather than another place where you could observe women with their hair uncovered. Just as Paul would not eat meat if it caused people to stumble, so women should cover their head to prevent unnecessary cultural shame. Covering her head did not make a woman more or less righteous: Christ's blood was all sufficient. But covering did speak of modesty and submission, which were cultural aspirations for a respectable Corinthian woman.

11:7

> *"A man ought not to cover his head, since he is the image and glory of God; but woman is the glory of man."*

When Jewish men came before God in prayer they covered their head with a prayer shawl, the Tallit. The custom most likely had it roots in the tassled garment of Num 15v39-40. But it wasn't to be a custom for those who follow Christ: they are to come before their holy God with a Christ-won confidence. In Christ they are acceptable image-bearers who bring glory to God. The second half of this verse needs careful reading given historical and cultural devaluing of women. Paul seems to be referring to the created order of Genesis 2v7 where it states that a man was created first. For a short time Adam stood preeminent in all of creation as the sole image-bearer. However, no suitable helper was found from the animals, so God put him into deep sleep and created a woman from his rib (Gen 2v22). It is in this sense that the woman is the glory of man: Adam was made from dust, but Eve was created from him. God brought life from life, created a woman from a man. Genesis 1v27 tells us male and female are created in the image of God and therefore in equal in personhood, value and dignity. Just as the Spirit brings glory to the Son and the Son to the Father; so wives bring glory to their husband, and husbands to God.

> *"This created order of equality and complementarity should be reflected in the public worship of the church in Corinth."*

11:8-9

> *"For man did not come from woman, but woman from man; neither was man created for woman, but woman for man."*

Because we read scripture across the distance of culture and many centuries, it is helpful to consider what the original readers understood this to mean. Given the Jewish heritage in the Corinthian church we can assume they would have known that God created Adam first. When no suitable helper was found for him, God put him into a deep sleep, took a rib from his side, and made a woman. Adam was given the authority to name her, initially calling her woman (Gen 2v23). However, after the fall and its curse, he renamed her with the hope-filled-name of Eve, the mother of all the living. The term 'helper' used in Genesis 2v18 means "one who supplies strength in the area that is lacking". The term does not imply the helper is stronger or weaker than the one helped. Eve is described as a helper fit for Adam she complements him, she makes up for what he is lacking. This created order of equality and complementarity should be reflected in the public worship of the church in Corinth.

11:10

> "It is for this reason that a woman ought to have authority over her own head, because of the angels."

Paul argues that a sense of propriety in worship is important because angels look on. Angels are created ministering spirits sent to serve those who inherit salvation (Heb 1v14). Hebrews 2v7 tells us that men and women were created a little lower than angels, yet these angelic beings submit to God and serve people. These loyal spiritual beings also observe the Corinthian church's worship. Paul wants these angels to see that men and women faithfully outwork God's pattern for His creation. For Corinthian wives who followed Jesus that meant that believing wives should wear a head covering as a symbol of their willing submission to God's (and their husband's) authority. Paul refers to angels watching elsewhere in the New Testament: "In the presence of God and of Christ Jesus and of the elect angels I charge you..." (1Tim 5v21).

11:11-12

> "Nevertheless, in the Lord woman is not independent of man, nor is man independent of woman. For as woman came from man, so also man is born of woman. But everything comes from God."

Paul continues by adding that there is to be interdependence between men and women. Husband and wife are more than just one flesh. Men and women are co-equal in personhood, value and worth. In the created order, Eve was made from Adam's rib, yet from then on, all men were born from a woman. Men and women are to live such that they have a mutual dependence on one another. They are to support each other physically, emotionally, spiritually and financially. The sexes are to have mutual reliance on and trust of one another. This is as true for single people as it is for married couples, although it will be worked out differently. God is trinity, three in one, so being made in God's image means being interdependent beings. This is how God has created us in His image as interdependent beings: marriage with headship, community with mutual dependence. Christians are to mirror this; we are to reflect God's dynamic interdependence for we are in the Lord.

> "God has created us in His image as interdependent beings: marriage with headship, community with mutual dependence..."

11:13

> *"Judge for yourselves: Is it proper for a woman to pray to God with her head uncovered?"*

Paul uses a rhetorical question: the implied answer is "no". Despite their factions (1v11), immorality (5v1), lawsuits (6v1), and confusion surrounding food sacrificed to idols (8v1), he assumes they will all agree on this. Because of the order built into Creation, and the angels who look on (v10), it should be obvious. A believing wife acknowledges she is under God's authority (and her husband's, by proxy), so she willingly practices the local expression of submission: a head covering. This young church face many complex issues (sexual immorality, lawsuits, arguments over apostles) yet Paul gives instruction on men, women and headcovering in worship. We do well to note the weight he gives to this issue: imaging God and expressing submission to His authority in worship was of great concern to Paul.

11:14-15

> *"Does not the very nature of things teach you that if a man has long hair, it is a disgrace to him, but that if a woman has long hair, it is her glory? For long hair is given to her as a covering."*

According to ESV Bible's study notes, the point Paul is making here is that men should look like men, as defined by local culture, and women should look like women, as defined by local culture. In so doing, this reflects the creation order and brings glory to both God and those made in His image. The strength of this interpretation is that it fits with the surrounding verses. Better still, it avoids introducing a practice for all believers in all cultures based on one isolated verse. Bad examples of this are the Mormon practice of baptism for the dead is taken from 15v29, and the Pentecostal extreme of drinking poison and handling snakes, taken from Mark 18v18. Navigating between timeless principles and temporary cultural expressions requires humility and leading by the Holy Spirit. One has to be open to the plain reading of the text AND an interpretation supported by the flow and verses of Scripture.

> *"Navigating between timeless principles and temporary cultural expressions requires humility and leading by the Holy Spirit."*

11:16 | *"If anyone wants to be contentious about this, we have no other practice—nor do the churches of God."*

According to Paul, women are to have a sign of authority on their heads and to wear their hair long; men are not to cover their heads and are to wear their hair short. Paul is emphatic that he and the other churches all follow these practices. But is this a timeless principle or a local practice that made sense to the original readers? It must be cultural, because:

1) There is no indication or clue as to what is "long" or "short": these are relative terms. Paul's point must be to promote distinction between sexes.
2) Anglican bishops wear hats as a sign of God given authority yet bear no cultural shame for their attire.
3) Paul often appeals to the timeless created order of male headship (indeed, this is a common thread through scripture), but there no such precedent for godly men to have short hair. On the contrary: Nazarites were set apart for God and wore long hair (Num 6v5); Samson was a Nazarite of God and his glorious strength was in his long hair (Jud 13v5).

"When necessary, good fathers need to cry 'foul play'."

11:17 | *"In the following directives I have no praise for you, for your meetings do more harm than good."*

The Corinthians' father in Christ (4v15) lovingly rebukes them - this is what fathers do (Heb 12v7). Not only do the people have divisions, lawsuits, sexual immorality and idolatry amongst them, but their gatherings do more harm than good! It is easy to wonder whether anything is going well in the Corinthian church. Yet Paul's opening remarks still stand. Inspired by God himself he says they are "sanctified in Christ Jesus, called to be holy" (1v2), that "Grace has been given them" (1v4) and that "He will keep you strong to the end" (1v8). The following directives are an outworking of grace, purposed to keep them strong until the end. A father's love sees beyond present shortfalls and focuses on who his children are and what they are to become. When necessary, good fathers need to cry 'foul play'. Whilst Paul has no praise for aspects of their gathered church life, his love for them is not in question. The same is true of their true Father in Heaven.

11:18

> *"In the first place, I hear that when you come to-gether as a church, there are divisions among you, and to some extent I believe it."*

Earlier in the letter Paul has mentioned that "some from Chloe's house-hold have informed me that there are quarrels among you" (1v11). He is referring to their divisions over the apostles they aligned with, be that Paul, Apollos, Cephas, or Christ. Paul has already mentioned the jealousy and quarrelling among them (3v3), as well as lawsuits (6v6). This social unrest is not restrained to the background gossip of people's homes, but spills out into the times they gather as a church. Paul believes some of what he has heard, although he allows room for exaggeration and misreporting by his source. He believes what he's being told 'to some extent'; it rings true given what he already knows or suspects. But he is choosing to believe the best about them. These are wise words for us to heed when hearing troubling reports about others.

> *"He is choosing to believe the best about them. These are wise words for us to heed when hearing troubling reports about others."*

11:19

> *"No doubt there have to be differences among you to show which of you have God's approval."*

Sadly, throughout the history of God's people, there have always been factions, divisions and differences. Often these would simply highlight whose hearts were fully devoted to the Lord and whose weren't. When Miriam and Aaron spoke against Moses it merely highlighted which of them had God's favour (Num 12v1). Whilst God has no favourites (Rom 2v11), He shows favour to those who turn to him with all their heart, mind, body and soul (Psa 119v2). Within the Corinthian factions only some had God's approval, and these arguments were a public way of singling them out. God is well able to redeem divisions for His purposes. Having "God's approval" is not to be confused with having right stand-ing before God - that is credited through faith in Christ alone (Rom 3v22). Rather, the approval Paul refers to is the approval given to those who exhibit mature Christian character and make good choices. Those who actions speak of love, unity and holiness are to be role models, ex-amples of Christian conduct for others to follow.

11:20-21

"So then, when you come together, it is not the Lord's Supper you eat, for when you are eating, some of you go ahead with your own private suppers. As a result, one person remains hungry and another gets drunk."

The Corinthians practised a form of the Lord's Supper but did not understand its true meaning. When they came together it revealed their divisions rather than affirming their unity. The Lord's Supper was supposed to demonstrate unity, sacrifice and Christ's character. In contrast, these believers did not wait for each other before starting to eat, and neither did they share their resources. Presumably those who were wise, noble and influential (1v26) had sufficient wine to get drunk, whilst the poor had nothing and could only look on at the feasting. Paul paints a picture of a church of two halves: one is self-centred, self-absorbed and has much, the others are little more than hungry spectators. Yes, everyone sat in the same room, but with no sense of regard for each other. It's little wonder that the Corinthians' meetings did more harm than good.

11:22

"Don't you have homes to eat and drink in? Or do you despise the church of God by humiliating those who have nothing? What shall I say to you? Shall I praise you? Certainly not in this matter!"

The Lord's Supper should have been an expression of unity and reconciliation between people of differing economic experiences. But the Corinthians' practice was a showcase of economic divides. The 'haves' were not providing for the 'have-nots', leaving the poor humiliated. Their communion was only about eating and drinking with those who were just like you. The Lord's Table had become a place of social snobbery; the wealthy had little regard for those who went hungry. This deeply troubles Paul, and he draws it to their attention. He refuses to affirm or praise this practice in their gatherings; he cannot and will not commend them in this. The church is to be the place where rich and poor come together, wait for each other, and express our unity.

> *"The church is to be the place where rich and poor come together, wait for each other, and express our unity."*

11:23-24

> "For I received from the Lord what I also passed on to you: The Lord Jesus, on the night he was betrayed, took bread, and when he had given thanks, he broke it and said, 'This is my body, which is for you; do this in remembrance of me.'"

Paul refers here to the last meal that Jesus had before he was arrested and crucified. Luke 22 v14-22 records how he gathered with the disciples in a large upper room, where they celebrated the passover with bread and wine. The Passover meal was both a memorial and a celebration, marking the miraculous exodus from slavery and looking to a coming kingdom. The Israelites weren't just liberated from slavery, they also escaped God's judgement. Every family had to be identified by the blood of a lamb to ensure their first born was not struck down (Exo 12). The meal also celebrated the provision of God, which sustained His people in their great Exodus. They were daily provided with manna from heaven. Miraculous though this was, it was all purposed to point forward to the true bread of life: Jesus. His body was broken to sustain God's people in our 'exodus' to the renewed heavens and earth.

11:25

> "In the same way, after supper he took the cup, saying, 'This cup is the new covenant in my blood; do this, whenever you drink it, in remembrance of me.'"

600 years before Jesus was born, the prophet Jeremiah spoke of a new covenant "Behold the days are coming, declares the Lord, when I will make a new covenant with the house of Israel and the house of Judah...I will put my law within them and write it on their hearts, I will be their God and they will be my people" (Jer 31v33). Jesus' life, death and resurrection were the proclamation and inauguration of this better covenant. This new way of relating to God was to be sealed by the blood of the Lamb of God. When followers of Jesus drink from the cup of wine, we are reminded of the sacrifice and the certainty of the basis of our relationship to God. We are to remember the Christ, the author and perfecter of our faith. He endured the cross, ignoring the fact it was a shameful death because of the joy set before Him, winning a people for Himself (Heb 12v2). Jesus' life, death and resurrection ushered in a new way or relating to God which is better by far. His blood provided complete - once for all - atonement for our sins: past, present, and future. Now that's worth remembering and celebrating.

> "His body was broken to sustain God's people in our 'exodus' to the renewed heavens and earth."

11:26

"For whenever you eat this bread and drink this cup, you proclaim the Lord's death until he comes."

The bread and wine help us to remember past events (the Exodus and then Christ's life, death and resurrection) and proclaim the future event of Christ's second coming. This meal looks both back and forwards. Looking forward to Christ's return is vital for Christian living. It brings hope for the future and certainty for the present. It makes sense of being faithful and of enduring through suffering. It speaks of a greater plan, that transcends our brief lives. It speaks of a certainty that triumphs, despite setbacks and death. Death could not hold him, and neither shall the future be able to restrain Him from returning: His day will come. Whenever we share bread and wine we proclaim the Lord's death: the Lamb of God was slain. By His blood we escape judgement and are released from slavery. We are sustained on our exodus by the "bread of life" (John 6v35) until He returns and eternally establishes His kingdom.

"Looking forward to Christ's return is vital for Christian living."

11:27

"So then, whoever eats the bread or drinks the cup of the Lord in an unworthy manner will be guilty of sinning against the body and blood of the Lord."

The Passover was to be eaten by the Israelites even if they were ceremonially unclean (Num 9v10). It was a means and a provision of grace. But under the new covenant, ratified with sacrificial blood, how you eat - your heart attitudes and outward behaviour - still mattered. The self-centeredness displayed in Corinthian meetings was wholly incompatible with the sacrificial nature of Christ. To act in these ways was contrary to Jesus' profound example, and was tantamount to sinning against Him. The unworthy manner no doubt included the arguments, divisions and lack of regard for the poor which was rampant in their meetings. Paul has already asked them not to associate with anyone who claims to be a brother or sister but is sexually immoral or greedy, an idolater or a slanderer, a drunkard or a swindler. They were not even to eat with such people (5v11). They were to ensure that communion was done in a manner that honoured Jesus, rather than sinned against Him.

11:28-29

"Everyone ought to examine them-selves before they eat of the bread and drink from the cup. For those who eat and drink without discern-ing the body of Christ eat and drink judgement on themselves."

To avoid 'sinning' against the body and blood of Jesus, Paul encourages the Corinthians to examine themselves before taking communion. Presumably he meant for them to confess and repent of selfishness and divisive behaviour. This is to be the precursor for communion, not a barrier to it. It requires that we humble ourselves and acknowledge both our shortfalls and our need of forgiveness. Feeding on Christ first requires a pause to allow for a sober self-assessment. Saints are works in progress, and depend upon the means of grace - they must not presume upon it. To participate in Lord's Table is to engage in a profound act of devotion. If it is done without earnest examination, the Lord will bring discipline to those who dishonour His Supper.

> *"Saints are works in progress, and depend upon the means of grace - they must not pre-sume upon it."*

11:30

"That is why many among you are weak and sick, and a number of you have fallen asleep."

Personal sin sometimes has grave physical consequences, as Ananias and Sapphira's story shows us (Acts 5v1-11). It's not that every sickness was a sign of God's disapproval. Timothy had a weak stomach, yet had a sincere faith and Paul regarded him as a true son (1 Tim 1v2, 5v23, 2 Tim1v5). Paul warns the Corinthians that they need to make changes: to stop eating the bread and drinking from the cup in an unworthy manner. This was for the good of both the gathered church and for their own physical well being. Some of their own number had died (the meaning of "fallen asleep", as in Matthew 27v52) because they brought God's discipline upon themselves. In Paul's mind, the reason behind some of their weakness and sickness was because God wanted to show who had His approval (v19). Not every sickness is a sign of God's disapproval. But if you are in bad relationship with fellow believers, your sickness may find its healing in forgiveness and restoration.

11:31

> *"But if we were more discerning with regard to ourselves, we would not come under such judgement."*

Paul is calling the believers in Corinth to make honest and continual assessments of themselves, and to make appropriate changes. As a result, they would not come under any judgement by God. Just as the captain of a sail boat keeps trimming the tiller to stay on course, so must they keep watching their lives. In so doing, they not only guard against going off course but also avoid strong discipline from the Lord. Given the context of a dysfunctional Lord's Supper, it is best understood that these believers should reflect on how they have sinned against one another and how to seek to make good their relationships. Repentance and seeking forgiveness are powerful agents of transformation. It is better that we judge ourselves than that we become weak, sick or even "fall asleep" (v30).

11:32

> *"Nevertheless, when we are judged in this way by the Lord, we are being disciplined so that we will not be finally condemned with the world."*

The Corinthians had got themselves in a mess concerning communion (amongst other things). They had brought judgement upon themselves. Some had become sick; some had died. But Paul states that God's discipline is not condemnation, but rather an act of mercy. Believers are justified through faith alone (Rom 5v16), and disciplined as children whom the Father loves and delights in (Pro 3v11-12). Their salvation is not brought into question; nonetheless, a change of behaviour is required. God's purpose is to bring many sons and daughters to glory, through the sufferings of the "author of their salvation" (Heb 2v10). Jesus is the one who sanctifies. By His example, the ongoing discipline of the Father, and the empowerment of the Spirit, we will not be condemned.

> *"Just as the captain of a sail boat keeps trimming the tiller to stay on course, so must they keep watching their lives."*

11:33

> *"So then, my brothers and sisters, when you gather to eat, you should all eat together."*

Paul concludes his reprimand by referring to them as brothers and sisters; they are joined by God as adopted siblings. Paul wants the best for them, just as a good father does for his children (4v15). Sadly their communion meals are characterised by impatience and division, hunger and feasting (19-22). What family doesn't wait for everybody to gather round the table? What family gives choice cuts to some members but not to others? What family allows some sibling to go hungry whilst others feast? Certainly this should not happen God's family. When they come together to eat, they should wait for everyone and ensure all have enough.

11:34a

> *"Anyone who is hungry should eat something at home, so that when you meet together it may not result in judgement."*

Sometimes our selfishness and appetites combine to create a toxic environment. This is what Paul is addressing here: hungry, self-centred Christ followers hijack the Lord's Supper. A sacrament becomes a train wreck. Paul's practical response is to remind them of the meaning of the meal,and to tell them to satisfy their hunger at home. Sometimes we simply need to meet our appetites - they're not wrong in themselves. But how and where we meet them is important. For Paul, love and unity must trump hunger. Hunger can be satisfied at home; love and unity must be expressed at the Lord's Table. Love eats at home and waits at church. This is a train wreck that can be avoided.

> ## *"Love eats at home and waits at church."*

11:34b | *"And when I come I will give further directions."*

Paul is not finished, nor has he exhausted his advice regarding how the Corinthians 'do' the Lord's Supper. But for now he has said 'enough' he will get to the other points when he visits them next. This is a clear reminder that he had an itinerant ministry that was both was fatherly and directive. Paul was less concerned with producing exhaustive lists and byelaws for each church and more concerned that they had the right teaching at the right time. He anticipated returning to them at some point, and would give further directions then. Given the factions in the church, as to which apostle they are following (1v12), this is a bold statement. In effect he is asserting "I am your father in Christ" (4v15): that he has the right to urge them to imitate him and follow his directives. Paul sends Timothy ahead of him; he will follow himself very soon (4v19).

> *"Paul was less concerned with producing exhaustive lists and byelaws for each church and more concerned that they had the right teaching at the right time."*

CHAPTER 12

12:1 | *"Now about the gifts of the Spirit, brothers and sisters, I do not want you to be uninformed."*

Paul moves on from instructions about how the Corinthians host the Lord's Supper to now begin a larger body of teaching on spiritual gifts. We can safely assume he is answering specific questions they had asked, just as he did on marriage, virgins, and food sacrificed to idols (7v1,v25 & 8v1). He does not want them to be uninformed about spiritual gifts; these are essential for believers, for the church to fulfil her mission. For Paul, these gifts are not optional, and should be used widely and wisely. They are distinguished from the fruit of the Spirit (Gal 5v22-23), in that the gifts are largely for the benefit of others, whilst the fruit is for personal sanctification (being made holy).

"Sinners prefer a silent authority."

12:2 | *"You know that when you were pagans, somehow or other you were influenced and led astray to mute idols."*

Paul refers to their old life as pagans in order to emphasise that most of them started life outside of the people of God. They were not born as Jews, nor did they grow up in a culture that acknowledged the one true God, Yahweh. Paul makes the point that they were led astray to worship mute idols. These idols either had nothing to say or they simply couldn't communicate. And yet pagans gave themselves to worship these mutes, despite their deafening silence. This was their shameful and foolish starting point in life; sinners prefer a silent authority. But now grace and peace have been given to them in Christ Jesus (1v4). Now, they are included in His household as beloved family members. Now they worship the God who speaks, and who gives spiritual gifts to His children.

12:3

> *"Therefore I want you to know that no one who is speaking by the Spirit of God says, 'Jesus be cursed,' and no one can say, 'Jesus is Lord,' except by the Holy Spirit."*

Those who were once led astray to worship mute idols need to be informed about the Spirit's activity. They were not used to a God who speaks to His people, and so were open to confusion and easily being misled. This would be especially true of the verbal spiritual gifts: prophecy and speaking in tongues. They had previously worshipped mute gods, but now had to contend with prayers in strange languages (tongues) and messages directly from God (prophecy). And this was not just from the recognised 'leaders', but from all believers, people just like themselves. So Paul equips these ex-pagans in the use of spiritual gifts. He seeks to bring clarity and discernment to their use, as well as a confidence and expectation that God will speak. The first thing Paul points out is that no-one who is empowered to speak by the Spirit of God will ever blaspheme Christ. Secondly, only those who have a genuine faith can say "Jesus is Lord", for this also is empowered by the Spirit.

12:4-6

> *"There are different kinds of gifts, but the same Spirit distributes them. There are different kinds of service, but the same Lord. There are different kinds of working, but in all of them and in everyone it is the same God at work."*

The ESV states that there are a variety of gifts, service, and activities, but the same God who empowers them in everyone. The purpose of these verses is not to distinguish between definitions of "gifts", "services" and "activities". Rather, it is to see all three as broad, encompassing terms that embrace a variety of God-empowered actions. All of these can be traced back to the grace of God and the the unity of God. The statements of diversity (gifts, service, activities) are unified, just as are the Son, Spirit, and Father, and bring unity for the common good. The Spirit gives and empowers. The Son calls to service. The Father prepares works and activities. The diversity of gifts within the Corinthian church is a reflection of the unity and diversity of the trinity. Corinthian unity can be strengthened if they appreciate each of their differing gifts and contributions.

> *"Corinthian unity can be strengthened if they appreciate each of their differing gifts and contributions."*

12:7

"Now to each one the manifestation of the Spirit is given for the common good."

To those who were known for their divisions, lawsuits, sexual immorality, and meetings which "did more harm than good", God gave spiritual gifts. These were gifts of grace, not merit. Everyone in this divided community was given the dignity of playing their part; none were overlooked. A manifestation is an event that clearly shows something that is otherwise abstract or theoretical. That fact that God exists and is a spiritual being is abstract in that it cannot be proved. So a "manifestation of the Spirit" means that a supernatural gift is given to all believers in order to clearly show both that God is amongst them and that He accepts them all (Acts 11v16-17). This manifestation was for the benefit and interest of the entire church. It was not to show who had God's approval amongst them - it was not restricted to only the mature or the deserving - but was given for the common good.

> *"Those who once worshipped mute idols are given verbal messages of wisdom and knowledge to speak on God's behalf."*

12:8

"To one there is given through the Spirit a message of wisdom, to another a message of knowledge by means of the same Spirit,"

Paul begins to list some of the many gifts given by the Spirit. The point must be illustrate variety and unity, as little detail of definition is given as to how they differ. We understand "wisdom" to be the quality of having experience and therefore being able to make a good judgement. By contrast, "knowledge" is more concerned with facts, information and understanding. According to the ESV study bible, the original Greek words "logos sophias" and "logos gnoseos" do not occur elsewhere in scripture, so it is difficult to be certain what they meant. But whatever the difference, those who once worshipped mute idols are given verbal messages of wisdom and knowledge to speak on God's behalf. The Spirit empowered some to speak wisely and others knowledgeably, all for their common good.

12:9

> *"to another faith by the same Spirit, to another gifts of healing by that one Spirit,"*

Whilst saving faith is indeed a gift from the Spirit (Eph 2v9), that is not the faith Paul has in mind here. This verse refers to the gift of faith that can move mountains (13v2) and see sick people healed (James 5v15). In Acts 14v9, a man crippled from birth had faith to be made well. When gifts of faith are used, people can be blessed directly or indirectly. Direct blessing occurs if they are the recipient of a healing or miraculous provision. Indirect blessing refers to being encouraged and strengthened by someone exercising their gift of faith. The Spirit also gives "gifts of healing" - note the plural, gifts . This suggests that people are not like Jesus, who healed numerous ailments; rather certain individuals were gifted for different kinds of healings. This would fit well with the theme of unity and diversity. Some may have a gift of healing for hearing, others a gift of healing for barrenness, and so on. Again, all such gifts are given by the Spirit for the common good.

> *"Paul mentions these spiritual gifts matter-of-factly, presumably because they were on display within their meetings."*

12:10

> *"to another miraculous powers, to another prophecy, to another distinguishing between spirits, to another speaking in different kinds of tongues, and to still another the interpretation of tongues."*

Paul mentions these spiritual gifts matter-of-factly, presumably because they were on display within their meetings. "Miraculous powers" most likely refers to the healings, signs and wonders which were part of New Testament church life. Simon, who practiced sorcery, followed Philip everywhere, astonished by the signs and miracles he saw (Acts 8v13). "Prophecy" refers to a Spirit-prompted utterance that has its roots in a revelation from God, but remains fallible because of the speaker's mediation of the revelation. As such, it should be tested - but not quenched or despised (1 Cor 14v29, 1 Thess 5v20). Because prophecy is a valued gift in church life, it is vital to be able to discern between spirits. The Satan, and the fallen angels that follow him, have always had an appetite to ape God's voice or offer a counterfeit influence. Tongues can be understood as speaking in a language that the speaker does not know, whether earthly or heavenly. The interpretation of such a language reverses the curse of Babel (Gen 11v9).

12:11

"All these are the work of one and the same Spirit, and he distributes them to each one, just as he determines."

The Spirit empowers and apportions as He sees fit, and in so doing local churches are strengthened. He brings unity through co-dependence: no one person will have all the gifts that a community needs. Jesus was the one exception. This work of the Spirit was not limited to the first few decades, in order for the New Testament church to be established; rather it is a pattern for church life until Christ returns. His people need these gifts manifestly amongst them in every generation of believers, regardless of their maturity or circumstances. The church will always need to see and experience the gifts of apostleship (1v11), healing, faith, wisdom, knowledge, prophecy and tongues. The Spirit liberally and sufficiently gives to bless and strengthen local churches. The interdependence of the differing gifts speak of the diversity and unity of God, as three persons yet being one.

12:12

"Just as a body, though one, has many parts, but all its many parts form one body, so it is with Christ."

Paul now refers to what he taught those in Rome: "For as in one body we have many members, and the members do not all have the same function, so we, though many, are one body in Christ" (Rom 12v4), and in Ephesus: "And he put all things under his feet, and gave him as head over all things to the church, which is his body" (Eph 1v22). He assumes the Corinthians are aware that the church is Christ's body: "And he is the head of the body, the church" (Col 1v18). Just as a body is unified but made up of many parts, so too is the church. Paul has listed a variety of gifts given to members of the church for the common good. These gifts are all to be in play, just as eyes, ears, hands, feet, lungs, stomachs, spleens and kidneys all need to function in their differing ways in order for the body to remain healthy.

> *"The church will always need to see and experience the gifts of apostleship (1v11), healing, faith, wisdom, knowledge, prophecy and tongues."*

12:13

> "For we were all baptised by one Spirit so as to form one body—whether Jews or Gentiles, slave or free—and we were all given the one Spirit to drink."

Paul reminds the Corinthians of the Spirit's central role: bringing unity to their diversity. The Spirit has come upon all believers, regardless of their ethnicity or social standing, and immersed them in Christ. The Spirit gives differing gifts which unify people. Now they are compelled by the Spirit to align their lives to Christ and His teaching. Water baptism symbolised the washing away of an old life, with the promise of a fresh start and a clean sheet. The Spirit comes first to regenerate and then bring life and power to this symbolism. This is true for all believers. The phrase "Jew and Greek, slave and free" is used to signal bookends of the full spectrum of people. All were given the one Spirit to drink: "If anyone thirsts, let him come to me to drink. Whoever believes in me, as the Scripture has said 'Out of his heart will flow rivers of living water'" (John 7v37-38).

12:14-15

> "Even so the body is not made up of one part but of many. Now if the foot should say, 'Because I am not a hand, I do not belong to the body,' it would not for that reason stop being part of the body."

People are people, and pride and envy lurks in all of our hearts. Paul continues the metaphor of a body in order to press home the challenge of acknowledging difference yet pursuing unity. Everyone knows a foot cannot exist apart from the body; but a foot is no less important for the functioning of the body than a hand. The absurdity of a foot claiming independence from a body, simply because it's not a hand, is laughable. And yet 'hand envy' is prevalent in almost every fellowship. Someone oftens wants to be as gifted in a similar way or role as someone else. But while it might be common - even understandable - that does not validate feelings of envy or discontentment. Just as the human body has been created by God with many parts, so too are local churches made up of many individuals. It is having the full complement of diverse parts that makes a healthy body.

> *"The Spirit has come upon all believers, regardless of their ethnicity or social standing, and immersed them in Christ."*

12:16

> *"And if the ear should say, 'Because I am not an eye, I do not belong to the body,' it would not for that reason stop being part of the body."*

Paul repeats the illustration for maximum effect; how absurd it would be for an ear to desire to be an eye, let alone to leave the body on account of this. It would be laughable if it wasn't such a familiar theme in church life. The fact that believers are gifted differently is undeniable, but that difference is vital for the church to be a healthy body. Difference does not sever connection but affirms interdependence. An ear might not value its gift of hearing but the body certainly benefits from its contribution. Differences in gifting, personality, and roles, can result in an individual withdrawing from the "body", but this is not a legitimate reason to do so. Hands, feet, ears and eyes all have contributions to make; all are missed if damaged or severed from the body. Their difference becomes their unique contribution, and the reason they enrich the whole. Whilst some parts of the church body are more visible, all parts belong and are needed.

> *"Their difference becomes their unique contribution, and the reason they enrich the whole."*

12:17

> *"If the whole body were an eye, where would the sense of hearing be? If the whole body were an ear, where would the sense of smell be?"*

The eye perceives light and converts it into electro-chemical impulses. It regulates intensity through a diaphragm, focuses it through an adjustable lens, converts the image, and transmits signals to the brain. It is incredible. The ear not only detects sound but also aids our sense of balance. Sound waves travel through the outer ear, are modulated in the middle ear, and are transmitted to the temporal lobe of the brain via the inner ear. This is brilliant. Both the eye and the ear are complex; they function differently, but both bring valuable contributions to the same body. The loss of either organ would negatively impact the body and would be registered as a disability in today's western culture. Paul's illustration is as powerful now as it was in the first century.

12:18 | *"But in fact God has placed the parts in the body, every one of them, just as he wanted them to be."*

Paul reminds the Corinthians that it is God's choice and design that ultimately matters. He is sovereign, good, and wise. He has shown great wisdom and care in designing the human body with all its intricacies and interdependence. Eyes and ears sit on top of a neck that can flex in order to give better sightlines and better detect where sounds comes from. Fingers are more sensitive than eyes because they have more receptors that can send signals to our brains. The digestive system utilises gravity as it breaks down food. All this has been arranged as He has chosen, and the Creator does not need to give an account to the Created. Each member of the body finds its purpose and meaning as part of the whole. Belonging to - and functioning within - the body is all because of God's will and His wise arrangement.

> *"All this has been arranged as He has chosen, and the Creator does not need to give an account to the Created."*

12:19-20 | *"If they were all one part, where would the body be? As it is, there are many parts, but one body."*

Paul urges the Corinthians to see the necessity of their differences. Neither the embalmed eyes or ears in a medical school laboratory constitute a body. It's diversity that make a body; a collection of similar body parts can only ever be a collection. Every part of the body contributes in different ways, but each part works for the common good. Each part is distinct, but each is vitally connected, and depends on the functioning of the whole. Paul pushes this point, presumably because of attitudes of inferiority and superiority amongst the believers. Paul urges them to acknowledge and value their unity (as one church body) and their diversity (they bring different gifts and contributions to the church body). If they were mainly a collection of arms (a metaphor for massive serving gifts within the church) but had no mouths (lacking in teaching gifts) they would not be a healthy body. Rather, they would simply be a macabre collection of body parts!

12:21

"The eye cannot say to the hand, 'I don't need you!" And the head cannot say to the feet, 'I don't need you!"'

Paul is working every angle, looking to remove any and every attitude that promotes disunity. He focuses on pride and arrogance. For the eye or head to say it has no need of other body parts is both foolish and arrogant. The eye can function without a hand, and the head can function without a foot, but the body overall would be limited in what it can do: it is dis-abled. For a Corinthian to lose a hand or foot because of an injury or infection, or even as a punishment, would be a significant setback. Their livelihood most likely depended upon these body parts. It would be unthinkable to say they had no need of them. The eye cannot honestly say to the hand "I don't need you!". It's not true, and simply reveals pride, arrogance, and superiority. And nothing chokes a sense of unity more than these.

12:22-24a

"On the contrary, those parts of the body that seem to be weaker are indispensable, and the parts that we think are less honorable we treat with special honor. And the parts that are unpresentable are treated with special modesty, while our presentable parts need no special treatment."

Paul continues by acknowledging that some parts of the body are more visible than others, such as the mouth and eyes, while other parts are less so. Paul argues that the presentable parts need no special treatment: they have enough profile and honour. Rather, the special honour should go to the hidden, "weaker" parts we think are less honourable. Verbal spiritual gifts, like prophecy and the speaking in and interpretation of tongues, can quickly command public honour when used wisely. Those with these gifts don't need special treatment. But those with the more hidden spiritual gifts, like serving, administration and helping others, do need special recognition. Though more hidden, their gifts are vital to the church and should be offered special honour to encourage their use and their users.

> *"Their livelihood most likely depended upon these body parts. It would be unthinkable to say they had no need of them."*

12:24b-25

"But God has put the body together, giving greater honor to the parts that lacked it, so that there should be no division in the body, but that its parts should have equal concern for each other."

Men and women, at their core, crave recognition and honour. But God uses honour to bring unity: all are to be honoured. When all are esteemed and thought well of, none are overlooked. God is working for unity in the body He has put together. He treats unpresentable parts with special modesty, thereby ensuring they are not exposed or shamed. The parts of the church body that we might be tempted to consider unworthy He treats with special honour. His desire is that each part of the church's body should have equitable concern for the other parts. The foot should be concerned for the hand, and the hand for the foot. Honour is to be used to convey our sincere concern for others. Unity is to be expressed through equal concern and care for the glory of God and the benefit of His people.

12:26

"If one part suffers, every part suffers with it; if one part is honored, every part rejoices with it."

Just as functioning eyes enable the body to act, so a broken foot negatively affects the body. It is the same with the local church - at least, it should be. A healthy church must have a way of feeling the pain, triumphs, joys, and setbacks of her members. How this is worked out and expressed will vary, but it must be worked out. Those within a church are to have a meaningful sense of belonging and interdependence. Good news is to be shared and rejoiced in. Setbacks and hardships are to be acknowledged and felt by the wider body. Whilst church size affects the way these things are expressed, the principle remains the same. This is true not just for local churches but also of the wider church body: the Protestants, Roman Catholics, and Eastern and Oriental Orthodoxy. Our understanding of the Church of God needs to be much wider than protestantism, and our interest in her not just piqued when hearing stories of persecution or revival. We are to rejoice and to suffer with one another.

> *"A healthy church must have a way of feeling the pain, triumphs, joys, and setbacks of her members."*

12:27

"Now you are the body of Christ, and each one of you is a part of it."

This statement is familiar to us but must have been remarkable to the Corinthians. The church is the physical representation of Christ in the world, in the sense that she joined to Christ, and follows Christ as her head. This understanding is consistent with all of Paul's writings. To the church in Ephesus he wrote "the church is his (Jesus') body" (Eph 1v23), and that apostles work to "equip the saints for the work of ministry, for building up the body of Christ" (Eph 4v12). To the believers at Colosse he wrote "for the sake of his body, that is, the church" (Col 1v24). And to those in Rome, Paul told: "so we, though many, are one body in Christ" (Rom 12v5). Being in Christ, being His body, is more than a spiritual address or identity. It has everything to do with a greater purpose. I am not my body, but my body hosts me; in the same way, Christ's presence is made manifest here through the church. His presence to believers, and to unbelievers, is through the church. Each believer plays a significant part in making His presence tangible.

> *"I am not my body, but my body hosts me; in the same way, Christ's presence is made manifest here through the church."*

12:28

"And God has placed in the church first of all apostles, second prophets, third teachers, then miracles, then gifts of healing, of helping, of guidance, and of different kinds of tongues."

Paul goes on to list some of the gifts given to Jesus' body in order for it to function in a healthy way. This rollcall is presumably in order of the importance or benefit to a local church. It is important to remember what was written just a few verses before: "presentable parts need no special treatment or greater honour", they are what they are. Apostles are first. As wise farmers they scatter good seed for a gospel harvest, and as master builders they lay a foundation on which to build churches (3v6, 10). Apostles and prophets work closely together, as Ephesians 2v20 records: "built on the foundation of the apostles and prophets with Christ Jesus himself as the chief cornerstone". This list of church 'body parts' is not exhaustive, but represents some of the gifts and functions needed for healthy church life.

12:29-30

"Are all apostles? Are all prophets? Are all teachers? Do all work miracles? Do all have gifts of healing? Do all speak in tongues? Do all interpret?"

Christ was the only one who had all the gifts. He alone is the true apostle, prophet, teacher, miracle worker, healer, etc. Only He had it all and could do it all. But He has ascended into heaven and we the church, are now His manifest presence here. However, no one person, or church, has all of Jesus' gifts and roles. It takes multiple healthy congregations to even begin to display something of the many roles, facets and gifts that Jesus brings to a community. So within a local church family, we can expect both a multiplicity of gifts but also a deficiency of certain gifts. This lack causes an appropriate dependance on other congregations to release what is needed. These verses give us permission and a framework to be local church working in close partnership with the wider church body. One point to note: a single congregation in isolation has a tendency to become a collection of 'preferred' body parts at the detriment of others.

> *"Within a local church family, we can expect both a multiplicity of gifts but also a deficiency of certain gifts."*

12:31

"Now eagerly desire the greater gifts. And yet I will show you the most excellent way."

In Paul's mind functions such as apostles, prophets, and teachers rank more highly than other gifts. The greater and higher gifts are those that build the church up, like prophecy (14v5). The goal is not to have the 'best' gift in order to receive personal accolade, but rather to seek the greater gifts for the benefit of others. Individual body parts are to look after their body. How these gifts are used is also important: prophecy must be done in love. Paul now goes on to speak of love as the highest motive and method. The way things are done in church life matters. Just getting the job done is not enough; how the job is done is equally important. There are bad ways and good ways; there are good ways and the most excellent way. The body of Christ has a characteristic way of moving, a signature tone of voice and manner of behaviour: that way is love.

CHAPTER 13

13:1 | *"If I speak in the tongues of men or of angels, but do not have love, I am only a resounding gong or a clanging cymbal."*

The Corinthians would have been familiar with gifted public speakers - it was part of their popular entertainment. What they weren't familiar with was the importance of love as the prime motive when exercising gifting in church life. Greeks used gongs in the context of battle, to rouse their troops for action or to instil fear in their enemies. Cymbals, likewise, were used to alert troops or to signal a new order. Speaking in church without love is like a signal gong without an army behind it; it promises much, but can deliver little, it is ineffectual in bringing the reign of a kingdom. Tongues announce, but it is love that delivers. If men and women pour forth speech without love, it is little more than a signal. It may announce that God is coming, but it is not the substance of His Kingdom: that only takes place through love.

> *"Without love, the gifted person has very little to offer the church family."*

13:2 | *"If I have the gift of prophecy and can fathom all mysteries and all knowledge, and if I have a faith that can move mountains, but do not have love, I am nothing."*

Prophecy and faith can be spectacular gifts. The prophetic powers alluded to here seem to be wider than just an encouraging contribution at a church meeting. Paul is suggesting an incredible God-given ability to understand mysteries, a gifting almost like Solomon's. The Jews and Greeks would have been tempted to highly esteem - if not to idolise - someone like that. But if this 'super Christian' did not have love, then Paul argues they are actually nothing. For Paul, love trumps gifting - even the spectacular gifts of faith, wisdom, knowledge, and prophecy. Paul argues that love should be the foundation that these gifts operate on. Without love, the gifted person has very little to offer the church family.

13:3

"If I give all I possess to the poor and give over my body to hardship that I may boast, but do not have love, I gain nothing."

God is love. Devotion to God is to have the motive of love: love for God and love for His people. So Paul argues that if you give all you possess to the poor, but your motive is not love, you gain nothing. Your resources have been distributed for the good of others, but your heart was not transformed. Your standing in the community may have gone up, but you'll have spent your wealth for nothing. If you follow the example of Shadrach, Meshach and Abednego who were willing to be thrown into a fiery furnace rather than deny their faith (Dan 3v17) but don't love fellow believers, the sacrifice counts for nothing. Love is the currency of God's kingdom; love is the key that unlocks us; love is to be the reason for our actions. God's household is to put on the family resemblance: love. God is not impressed by charitable works, rather, He desires that we love one another as He has loved us (John 13v34). We are to be known primarily for our love for each other, not for our zeal or charity.

13:4

"Love is patient, love is kind. It does not envy, it does not boast, it is not proud."

This passage on love is often read at weddings, but it's originary purpose is as an address to a church family that is zealous in exercising spiritual gifts but relationally fragmented. Paul urges them to see themselves as one body, and to work to build one another up. Their motives and attitudes must be love. Love is patient: it waits for each other at the Lord's Supper, and even chooses to eat at home if that help to be patient. Love is kind: it shares food with one another so that none go hungry, addressing the concerns of 11v21. Envy says "I want what you have" - be that their father's wife (5v1) or to be gifted like another (12v5). Love does not boast by declaring allegiance to the supposed 'super apostles' (4v6, 3v21). Love is not arrogant or proud, love does speaks against Paul in his absence (4v18-19).

> *"Love is the currency of God's kingdom; love is the key that unlocks us; love is to be the reason for our actions."*

13:5

"It does not dishonour others, it is not self-seeking, it is not easily angered, it keeps no record of wrongs."

Some things are best understood in relation to what they are not. Love is not rude: it is not disrespectful or sharp with others, it does not insist on its own way, it is not irritable. Love is not easily angered: it seeks to rise above circumstances. When love is present strong feelings of displeasure can be acknowledged but managed with restraint. There may be anger but there is never rage (uncontrolled aggression). Love keeps no record of wrongs, nor is it resentful. When love is predominant, feelings of bitterness and indignation diminish. Love takes its lead from Jesus' example in Gethsemane: "Yet not as I will, but as you will" (Matt 26v39).

> ## *"Love may experience or endure evil, but it will never delight in it."*

13:6

"Love does not delight in evil but rejoices with the truth."

We would do well to remind ourselves that the Corinthians boasted that a man had his father's wife (5v1), and revelled in their divisions (1v12). Paul argues that love does not celebrate wrongdoing, but rejoices with truth. He echoes here the Proverbs: "A fool finds pleasure in evil conduct but a man of understanding delights in wisdom" (Pro 10v23). By definition, nothing good can come from evil; its consequences are always that which is morally wrong, and it causes harm and injury. Love may experience or endure evil, but it will never delight in it. Rather, love rejoices with the truth; love celebrates kindness, mercy, holiness, sacrifice, and patience. Love delights in the moral goodness laid out in God's word, which is His wisdom and Law. Love celebrates light. Love delights in Jesus. Love cheers loudly when the gospel takes root.

13:7

"It always protects, always trusts, always hopes, always perseveres."

Paul is showing the Corinthians the most excellent way; because love bears all things, love chooses to endure. Paul told the Colossians to clothe themselves with compassion, kindness, humility, gentleness and patience. Bear with each other and forgive whatever grievance [...] put on love, which binds them all together in perfect unity" (Col 3v12-14). Despite the differences between the people in Corinth, even their divisions, they are to believe and hope for the best of each other. When love chooses to trust and to hope, nothing and no one can shipwreck the outcome. Given their context, this must have seemed like idealism at its best. Has Paul not understood the nature and depth of the divisions and misunderstanding among them? He has - but he also knows that love demands forgiveness and rejects cynicism. Love does not give up on people, but binds them together in unity.

> *"That is why love is the most excellent way: love transcends death."*

13:8

"Love never fails. But where there are prophecies, they will cease; where there are tongues, they will be stilled; where there is knowledge, it will pass away."

The ESV says "love never ends". This feels like the concluding statement of verses 4-7: love always trusts, hopes, endures... love never ends, so it never fails. Paul contrasts this summary of love, which is a fruit of the Spirit, with the gifts of the Spirit such as prophecy, tongues and knowledge (12v7-11). Prophesying will cease, as will speaking in tongues and giving words of knowledge. These are temporary gifts for this age. By contrast, love will endure death and be present in the age to come. That is why love is the most excellent way: love transcends death. These verses are not an argument for a cessationist view of the charismatic gifts, that is not Paul's intention. Rather, he is contrasting the gifts for this world to the higher way of love.

13:9-10

"For we know in part and we prophesy in part, but when completeness comes, what is in part disappears."

Paul continues arguing for the most excellent way; love endures, and therefore is the greater gift. Those who prophesy, or who have the gift of knowledge, do so with limitation. They do not have the full revelation from God, and are liable to mishear or misinterpret the message. But when Jesus returns, when completeness comes, the imperfect hearing of timely utterances from God will be replaced by hearing from Him perfectly, face to face, as the created before our Creator. Prophecy and knowledge are gifts to use as we await Christ's second coming. When He returns, the need for these gifts will disappear, since there will be no sin to cloud God's will. So prophecies will cease (they will be fulfilled), messages from God through others will be stilled (as we shall be able to talk face to face), and the knowledge that we have will pass away (superseded by a renewed heavens and earth).

13:11

"When I was a child, I talked like a child, I thought like a child, I reasoned like a child. When I became a man, I put the ways of childhood behind me."

Here Paul speaks of progression; the speech, thought and reason of a child changes as the child matures. Childish ways are appropriate for those awaiting adulthood. In the same way, gifts of prophecy, tongues and knowledge are like childish ways, in that they will be put aside when we come into adulthood - picture language for when Christ returns. Paul wants the Corinthians to see that the 'spectacular' verbal gifts they treasure are only temporary. Just as the speech and reasoning of a child appears limited compared to that of a mature adult, so will the gifts of prophecy, tongues and knowledge appear limited compared to the glory of the age to come. These childlike ways are appropriate for a season, but they will be superseded at the coming of Christ. But love is never put behind us.

> *"These childlike ways are appropriate for a season, but they will be superseded at the coming of Christ."*

13:12

"For now we see only a reflection as in a mirror; then we shall see face to face. Now I know in part; then I shall know fully, even as I am fully known."

These verses are an explanation of verses 9 to 10. The Corinthians are living with the imperfect as they await the perfect. Paul uses the metaphor of an ancient mirror, made from polished metal. The reflection offered by these was dim, unlike modern glass mirrors with their silver coating. The Corinthians could only see the glory of God as though they were looking at a dim reflection in a bronze mirror. But one day they would see clearly, as though looking at someone face to face. When that day happens, in the form of Christ's second coming, spiritual gifts like prophecy, tongues and knowledge will be superseded. Then the Corinthians shall see God face to face, up close and personal. No longer will they have to reply on faith or a dim reflection in a poor mirror. Then they will encounter Him in such a way that they will fully know that Jesus is Lord, and will be assured that He knows them fully.

13:13

"And now these three remain: faith, hope and love. But the greatest of these is love."

Paul sums up his letter's 'diversion' on love by stating the three great virtues of the Christian message: faith, hope, and love. He has been looking forward to the day when perfection comes (v10); when we will see God face to face and will know fully. That day requires faith: being sure of what we hope for, and certain of what we do not yet see. The object of that faith is Christ. Faith in Him leads us to hope in His second coming. It is a sure and certain hope that a renewed heaven and earth will reveal the perfection of Christ and us in Him. Love is the greatest quality because it is the very essence of God (1 John 4v8). In love there is no fear, for whoever abides in love abides in God (1 John 4v16-17). Love brings confidence for the day of judgement. And love was the reason that God gave His only begotten Son, "that whoever believes in Him should not perish but have everlasting life" (John 3v16). So the greatest of these virtues is love.

> *"Then they will encounter Him in such a way that they will fully know that Jesus is Lord, and will be assured that He knows them fully."*

CHAPTER 14

14:1 | *"Follow the way of love and eagerly desire gifts of the Spirit, especially prophecy."*

The Corinthians had been elevating certain spiritual gifts above others, resulting in division and conflict. In chapter 12 Paul begins to address this by stressing the diversity of spiritual gifts given by God to the church, whilst also emphasising that the church is one body. He continues in chapter 13 by focusing on love, the motivation for using all gifts. First he turns his thoughts to how these gifts should be used in the church's gatherings. They are gifts from God - even though their misuse has caused division. As such they are not to be dumbed down or rejected but earnestly desired - the people are to practise a strong, intense conviction. This applies especially to the gift of prophecy. Paul will go on to explain the reasons for this, clear, strong encouragement to single out the gift of prophecy for prolific use. Our God is not a mute pagan idol who can't speak to His people (12v2). And what is Paul's first statement on this issue of gifting? That the most excellent way to receive a spiritual gift is when it is packaged in love.

> *"The most excellent way to receive a spiritual gift is when it is packaged in love."*

14:2 | *"For anyone who speaks in a tongue does not speak to people but to God. Indeed, no one understands them; they utter mysteries by the Spirit."*

Paul begins by contrasting the gift of tongues (speaking in other languages) with that of prophecy. Tongues is a prayer language, a means of communicating with God, and as such it is directed towards God. The gift of tongues is a God-given means for the human spirit to communicate with God by the Spirit of God. It is not a means of speaking to others; it is not a holy language used to talk to other believers. The intended audience is God. Indeed, anyone who hears an uninterpreted tongue has no idea what is being said; the speaker is uttering mysteries in the Spirit. Mystery is best thought of here as things that are as yet unknown, hidden or disclosed, as opposed to impossible or very difficult to explain. God's secret wisdom has been sought out by the Spirit of God (1 Cor 2v7,10). That same Spirit dwells in us and helps us to pray.

14:3

> *"But the one who prophesies speaks to people for their strengthening, encouraging and comfort."*

Whereas the one who speaks in a tongue speaks to God in words that no-one understands, the one who prophesies speaks to fellow people in words that are easily understood. Prophecy functions to strengthen, to build believers up and to bring them consolation. It acts to bless, bring courage and hope, as though Christ himself were in the room speaking. The contrast Paul sets up is to demonstrate why the Corinthians should especially desire the gift of prophecy above other gifts. Their church had divisions and serious issues; to anticipate Paul's later metaphor of a body, it needed healing. Prophecy, when rightly packaged in love, builds people up and brings them together. Prophecy should bring confidence, hope and unity.

Its purpose is to strengthen, comfort and encourage; it must be rooted in love. We know that prophetic words can also bring warning or challenge (Acts 21v11) but that is not Paul's focus here.

14:4

> *"Anyone who speaks in a tongue edifies themselves, but the one who prophesies edifies the church."*

To 'edify' means to 'strengthen'. Its original meaning refers to building a house: it signifies active participation, not something that is passively done to you. Edification involves helping one another along the road to Christ-likeness. Paul uses this idea to show why prophecy is preferable to tongues: prophecy edifies, it builds up the church. Prophecy is a means to help others walk along the path to deeper spiritual maturity. Notice that Paul prioritises the building up of the church collectively rather than individually. Given their deep divisions and factions, this was clearly deliberate. Paul urges the Corinthians to participate in the way of love and especially to desire to build the church up (v1). They are to prophesy in such a way that everyone better understands who God is, and more closely follows Christ.

> *"Edification involves helping one another along the road to Christ-likeness."*

14:5

> *"I would like every one of you to speak in tongues, but I would rather have you prophesy. The one who prophesies is greater than the one who speaks in tongues, unless someone interprets, so that the church may be edified."*

Paul wants the Corinthians to pursue spiritual gifts in their meeting; he doesn't want these gifts silenced or dumbed down. He would like every one of the Corinthians to speak in tongues, but if he had to choose between the gifts he would prefer for them to prophesy. Here Paul appropriates their familiar but flawed hierarchical thinking - their conversations about "who is the greatest" or "what is the best gift" - to his own advantage. He states that the one amongst them who builds up the church is greater than the one who speaks to God! Given that prophecy is God speaking to strengthen, encourage and comfort his people, prophecy trumps uninterpreted tongues. However, if tongues are interpreted for the people to understand, the church can be edified by hearing this Spirit-inspired prayer and praise towards God. Both prophecy and interpreted tongues place God's people in active dialogue with their Father. And both must be used in 'the most excellent way': motivated by love. These spiritual gifts are to be encouraged in church gatherings, because when they are used properly they benefit the body of Christ.

> *"Edification requires more than just listening or spectating: it comes through understanding."*

14:6

> *"Now, brothers and sisters, if I come to you and speak in tongues, what good will I be to you, unless I bring you some revelation or knowledge or prophecy or word of instruction?"*

All of Paul's advice is motivated by love: he was aiming to strengthen the church. To speak in a tongue in a public setting, with no interpretation, may make the speaker look spiritual - even impressive - but it does not benefit the listening saints. Unless there is an interpretation in an intelligible language, the people literally have no idea what the speaker has said. Paul then lists more examples of forms of public speech that benefit the listening church: - 'revelation', 'knowledge', 'prophecy' and 'word of instruction' - though this list is not exhaustive or definitive. Edification requires more than just listening or spectating: it comes through understanding. Simply hearing a tongue does not bless or edify the hearers, although the speaker edifies himself (v4).

14:7

"*Even in the case of lifeless things that make sounds, such as the flute or harp, how will anyone know what tune is being played unless there is a distinction in the notes?*"

In order to illustrate the advantages of understanding something that is said compared with merely witnessing uninterpreted tongues, Paul turns to common instruments of his day: the flute and harp. Paul's argument is that if these objects can be used to play distinct and intelligible notes, how much more should spirit-filled, living people speak distinct, understandable words. Just as a tune needs to be distinct in order to be recognised and so to bring blessing to the listener, so too should tongues and prophecy be understood in order to bless and edify those who hear them. The skill of the musician is to make distinct notes and combine these into a recognisable tune. Paul uses this familiar image to illustrate the importance of understanding as a principle for using spiritual gifts in church life.

> "*Just as a tune needs to be distinct in order to be recognised and so to bring blessing to the listener, so too should tongues and prophecy be understood in order to bless and edify those who hear them.*"

14:8

"*Again, if the trumpet does not sound a clear call, who will get ready for battle?*"

Trumpets and bugles were used in the ancient world to signal an alarm or to rally people together. This imagery would have been familiar to the Corinthians; an equivalent for us might be the much like the familiar bugle call of the US cavalry in cowboy movies of yester-year. Jeremiah 4 describes the anguish of hearing the sound of the trumpet, the alarm for war. Ezekiel 33 talks of the watchman who sees 'the second coming' and blows the trumpet to warn the people (Eze 33v3). After God's people left Egypt and entered the desert wilderness, trumpets were used to summon and coordinate the tribes (Num 10v1-8). It was vital that this call to get ready was sounded clearly; it had to be distinct and recognisable. The trumpet call had to be understood so the hearers knew what to do. They needed to be able to discern what was expected of them by their commanding officer. A muffled call was no good to anyone; worse, it could potentially be disastrous.

14:9

> *"So it is with you. Unless you speak intelligible words with your tongue, how will anyone know what you are saying? You will just be speaking into the air."*

Just as the trumpet should clearly sound the call for battle, so should the use of spiritual gifts sound a clear message of edification. Public speech in church meetings should be intelligible and should strengthen its hearers. We can only guess at the circumstances Paul is addressing, but it seems that tongues were commonly spoken in their meetings but were not interpreted. These spectacular verbal addresses may have appeared impressive, but no-one understood what was going on! Simply speaking in an unintelligible tongue in a church meeting does no good (v6). At best the Corinthians were simply speaking to God and edifying themselves; at worst they were reinforcing divisions between the established and the new believers. Paul is writing to help the Corinthians navigate away from this chaotic practice. Just as instruments are played carefully to produce intelligible notes, so too should spiritual gifts be used wisely to bring intelligible encouragement.

14:10

> *"Undoubtedly there are all sorts of languages in the world, yet none of them is without meaning."*

Paul continues to press his point by using a different illustration: human languages. As an educated Jew he would have spoken multiple languages including Greek, Hebrew and Aramaic. He understood that languages help people to communicate and connect with one another. In the same way, the gift of tongues is a language to help people to connect to and communicate with God. When the gift of tongues is used, it is primarily directed towards God; it is a language to help us to pray. As such we should expect it to have a wide vocabulary to help us express our every emotion, need and aspiration. It should not consist of random sounds or phrases that have been learnt and are endlessly repeated. When exercised over time, the language of tongues will develop. It will also have its own cadence and grammar.

> *"Just as instruments are played carefully to produce intelligible notes, so too should spiritual gifts be used wisely to bring intelligible encouragement."*

14:11

> *"If then I do not grasp the meaning of what someone is saying, I am a foreigner to the speaker, and the speaker is a foreigner to me."*

God's church is a multinational, multi-ethnic family who are called together to express God's manifold wisdom. Those who were once foreigners and strangers to each other are brought together in Christ; they are joined in heart and become kin. As such, behaving in a way that excludes or can't be understood is not appropriate. If a tongue is prayed but not interpreted, people will be alienated and discouraged. In the same way that a foreigner who can't understand a local conversation is excluded, an uninterpreted tongue excludes those who hear it. Paul's concern is not that someone has spoken in a tongue but that its meaning cannot be grasped by others. Brothers and sisters in Christ are not to remain foreigners to one another; tongues are supposed to edify not to expose divides. Spiritual gifts should be used to unite a church.

14:12

> *"So it is with you. Since you are eager for gifts of the Spirit, try to excel in those that build up the church."*

Just as musicians need lots of practice in order to play discernible notes, and just as it is vitally important for a signal trumpet to give a clear call, and just as a foreign language needs to be understood in order to connect people, so should the Corinthians practise spiritual gifts in a way that strengthens and brings the church together. A flute played badly or in an unrecognisable manner does not feed the soul of its hearers. It is worth noting again that Paul affirms the Corinthians' eagerness for spiritual gifts, despite the difficulties the church was experiencing. He encourages them to excel in the gifts that build up the church. The end goal that he has in mind is a unified and healthy church. Spiritual gifts are simply a God-given means to achieve this end.

> *"Paul's concern is not that someone has spoken in a tongue but that its meaning cannot be grasped by others."*

14:13

"For this reason the one who speaks in a tongue should pray that they may interpret what they say."

The 'reason' this verse refers to is from the preceding sentence: to 'build up the church'. Because the driving motive is not just to say a prayer, but to edify those who are listening, anyone speaking in tongues in a church meeting should also ask God for an interpretation of what they have prayed out. The person who speaks the tongue should take primary responsibility for its interpretation. In this sense, a prayer said in tongues is incomplete (in terms of edifying the church) until it can be understood by those listening. When this spectacular oratory gift is used in church meetings it should be accompanied by a silent prayer for the interpretation. Although the interpretation can come from someone else, the original speaker should still pray for the interpretation. Love demands that the body of believers is built up, not that one person's gift is elevated.

> *"In this sense, a prayer said in tongues is incomplete until it can be understood by those listening."*

14:14

"For if I pray in a tongue, my spirit prays, but my mind is unfruitful."

Paul goes on to make a distinction between his mind and his spirit. His mind is the element of his being that enables him to think and to process the physical world around him. His spirit is the invisible, internal element of his being, the essence of who he is, the source of his emotion and character, and the part of him that is tuned into an awareness of God. Paul is saying that when he prays in a tongue his spirit is engaged but his intellect is not. He is uttering mysteries using his spirit that have not yet been disclosed to his mind (14v2). Remember the context of this statement: he is arguing that for the church to be built up they must be able to understand what is being said. Our minds need to be renewed in order for us to be transformed (Rom 12v2). Our minds need to be able to test what is spoken in order to discern the will of God and to know what is good. Speaking in tongues employs the spirit of a person but leaves their mind idle. But our minds need to be engaged if transformation is to occur.

14:15

> *"So what shall I do? I will pray with my spirit, but I will also pray with my understanding; I will sing with my spirit, but I will also sing with my understanding."*

Paul acknowledges two aspects to himself: his spirit and his mind. He wants both to be engaged in the things of God. He is seeking to marshal all of himself in his devotion to God and the use of the gifts given to him. Rather than pray in a tongue, where his spirit is active but his mind is unfruitful, his preference would be to engage all of himself. We are not to pray or sing to God in tongues and let our mind drift off to something else - an experience common to all charismatics! Whenever we are praying or singing in tongues we should be fully engaged with all of our being, as we best we can. The heavenly prayer language should not be reduced to a meaningless chant that unconsciously tumbles out of our mouths whilst we look around a room. Using the gift of tongues to pray or sing praise to God is not to be done half- heartedly or mechanically. Singing and praying in tongues requires effort and intention. Then, and with interpretation, it will build up both the speaker and the wider church.

14:16

> *"Otherwise when you are praising God in the Spirit, how can someone else, who is now put in the position of an inquirer, say 'Amen' to your thanksgiving, since they do not know what you are saying?"*

Paul asks the Corinthians to consider a hypothetical - albeit likely - situation to illustrate his point. He envisages a member of their congregation using the gift of tongues (colloquially referred to here as 'in the Spirit') to give praise to God, and someone else in the congregation to be an 'inquirer'. This most likely describes someone who is interested in the Christian faith: Corinthians, like most Greeks at the time, loved to hear new ideas. This outsider is looking in, maybe exploring the faith, but would be unable to make sense of the prayer spoken in tongues. Therefore they could not meaningfully agree with what is said, or 'say "Amen"' to the thanksgiving. They would not be helped in their understanding of the Christian faith or be encouraged by what was spoken.

It is important to note that tongues are not to be banned from church meetings on the basis of being sensitive to visitors; rather, tongues are to be included and interpreted. We will see more on that subject later.

> *"We are not to pray or sing to God in tongues and let our mind drift off to something else - an experience common to all charismatics!"*

14:17 | *"You are giving thanks well enough, but no one else is edified."*

Paul continues to press home the need for thanksgiving to be intelligible. Thanksgiving has two aims: firstly, to give honour and recognition to God for what He has done, and secondly to encourage others in their faith by declaring what God has done. Giving thanks to God in a manner that can't be understood by others forgets the important second aim, edification of the church. Chapter 13 teaches that love is needed: love seeks to glorify God, and love looks for every opportunity to build people up. Love desires to encourage fellow believers by testifying about what God has done and is doing in lives today. Unintelligible thanksgiving robs fellow believers of hearing about God's provision and faithfulness; it is like a tune being played but the notes are indistinguishable (v7). Unintelligible thanksgiving prevents inquirers from hearing faith-giving accounts of God's mercy and provision for people just like them.

> *"Unintelligible thanksgiving robs fellow believers of hearing about God's provision and faithfulness;"*

14:18-19 | *"I thank God that I speak in tongues more than all of you. But in the church I would rather speak five intelligible words to instruct others than ten thousand words in a tongue."*

Paul had lived and worked among the Corinthians for 18 months when he planted the church (Acts 18). His spiritual gifts and the way he used them would have been familiar to many of the congregation. Presumably they already knew his zeal for speaking in the Spirit; that's why he can say with confidence that he "speaks in tongues more than all of you". They observed his zeal but they missed his motive to always build people up. Church gatherings are not supposed to be a showcase for spiritual gifts, they are a place to strengthen others using spiritual gifts. Five intelligible words that instruct and help fellow believers are more preferable than a long outburst of an unintelligible tongue. So whilst Paul affirms the gift of tongues as a personal prayer language that edifies the believer (14v4) and that - when it is interpreted - can edify the whole church (14v5), he prefers the trumpet to give a clear call (14v8): a short trumpet blast of intelligible notes will instruct the troops to get ready (14v8).

14:20 | "Brothers and sisters, stop thinking like children. In regard to evil be infants, but in your thinking be adults."

Whilst Jesus affirmed childlike faith (Matt 19v14), Paul reprimands the Corinthians because they are still thinking like children: they are mere infants in Christ (3v1). Children have little concern for others and are centred on their own needs. But Paul wants the Corinthians to be mature, to be skilled in righteous living, to place the concerns of others front and centre in their use of their gifts. Their use of spiritual gifts - especially tongues - is childlike in the sense that it demonstrates their lack of concern for others. Hebrews 5v13 says that those who live on milk - that is, infants - are "unskilled in righteousness". That said, he does want the Corinthians to remain infants in regard to evil; he wants them to continue unskilled and immature in their wickedness. Paul exhorts them to be underdeveloped in sexual immorality, idolatry, youthful passions, the love of money, craving for controversy, envy, dissension and pride - to name but a few things.

> "When a tongue is spoken but is not interpreted, it enacts judgment by excluding people from the blessing of God."

14:21 | "In the Law it is written: 'With other tongues and through the lips of foreigners I will speak to this people, but even then they will not listen to me, says the Lord.'"

Paul refers to the 'Law', the Torah, and specifically Isaiah 28v11-12 - although this is not an exact quote. This passage in Isaiah describes judgement to be brought on Ephraim, the northern kingdom. God will speak against this fading kingdom by using strange and foreign languages that they cannot understand. This has echoes of the curses for disobedience in Deuteronomy 28v49, where God brings judgement to bear against His people using a "hard-faced nation whose language you do not understand". This is a fulfilment of the curse of Babel, of not being able to understand what is being said (Gen 11v9).

Paul's point is that not being able to understand is often an expression of judgement by God (Matt 13v13). When a tongue is spoken but is not interpreted, it enacts judgement by excluding people from the blessing of God. By contrast, love always seeks to use spiritual gifts to build people up, to include and to bless them.

14:22

> *"Tongues, then, are a sign, not for believers but for unbelievers; prophecy, however, is not for unbelievers but for believers."*

In this verse Paul gives a statement about two signs in public meetings; over the next few verses he explains what the signs mean. Uninterpreted tongues is a sign of judgement against unbelievers. Prophecy is a sign of God's blessing on believers. It is worth noting that this presupposes that unbelievers (outsiders or inquirers) are present in the church's meetings. The church is to be open to unbelievers, be they sceptics, earnest seekers, or anyone in between. They should be free to observe and take part in most aspects of corporate worship. They are free to observe and experience the gifts of the Holy Spirit in action. They will see signs, both positive and negative, that speak of a living and dynamic God not a mute idol (12v2). These signs speak of something more than clever teaching or eloquent speech (1v22). Tongues and prophecy speak to the gathered community; they are signs that divide sheep from goats (Matt 25v32-34). As such, they must be used wisely.

14:23

> *"So if the whole church comes together and everyone speaks in tongues, and inquirers or unbelievers come in, will they not say that you are out of your mind?"*

Acts 2 records the Holy Spirit coming upon the apostles, filling them and enabling them to speak in other languages (Acts 2v1-6). This had a mixed effect upon those who heard it: God-fearing Jews were amazed and perplexed and asked one another "what does this mean?". Others, however, made fun of the apostles and said "they have had too much wine" (Acts 2v12-13). Against this backdrop, Paul sees uninterpreted tongues as a negative action against outsiders, unbelievers and those who do not understand. They may conclude that Christians are out of their minds and leave the church. Yes, people will always find offence in the gospel, yet Paul urges the Corinthians to do all they can to love their fellow citizens, the outsiders and the unbelievers. Whilst outsiders may mock and ridicule the gathered church, it shouldn't be because the church has acted immaturely.

> *"The church is to be open to unbelievers, be they sceptics, earnest seekers, or anyone in between."*

14:24-25a

> "But if an unbeliever or an inquirer comes in while everyone is prophesying, they are convicted of sin and are brought under judgement by all, as the secrets of their hearts are laid bare."

Exodus 8v22-23 records that during the plague of flies, God would make a visible distinction between His people and others, so that all would know that the Lord was in the land. This was in the context of Moses telling Pharaoh to release God's people. There, prophecy functioned to show on whom God's blessing rests and who are outsiders. It is an expression of both God's love and righteous judgement, and one that all could understand. It is the same when God's people prophesy in the presence of unbelievers. It demonstrates that God is in the land but that they are currently separated from Him and excluded from His blessing. However, words of knowledge (12v8) spoken in their own language will lay the secrets of their hearts bare. Similarly, the Spirit may bring personal conviction of sin, or illuminate their sins when the unbeliever considers themselves. Through prophecy the unbeliever is able to understand their condition and able to repent.

14:25b

> "So they will fall down and worship God, exclaiming, 'God is really among you.'"

Prophecy, when handled maturely, has two positive outcomes. Firstly, believers are strengthened, encouraged and comforted (14v3). Secondly, unbelievers or enquirers will see it as a sign of God's blessing upon the church and will proclaim, with the Spirit's help, that "God is really among you". Prophecy is also a means of demonstrating that God is real, and when used maturely - can powerfully penetrate the hearts of men and women. The obvious question to ask is whether we see this in RFC meetings - or even whether we want to see this? Paul has written to ensure that prophecy is used wisely in church gatherings in Corinth. We can safely assume it should be playing a part in our meetings as well. It is interesting to note that God often used prophecy to signal those on whom His favour rested: Saul prophesied after being anointed as King by Samuel (1 Sam 10v10); David prophesied amongst the prophets at Naioth in Ramah (1 Sam 19v20); Joel prophesied that sons and daughters and men and women would prophesy (Joel 2v28-30).

"Through prophecy the unbeliever is able to understand their condition and able to repent."

14:26

"What then shall we say, brothers and sisters? When you come together, each of you has a hymn, or a word of instruction, a revelation, a tongue or an interpretation. Everything must be done so that the church may be built up."

This is one of the very few descriptions of what an early church meeting looked like. It matters little whether this is from Paul's memory of the meetings, or his expectation, or as described by those from Chloe's household (1v11). What is clear is that multiple people are bringing a variety of contributions; the list is not to be thought of as exhaustive or definitive. The point is that these contributions were purposed to build up the church, to strengthen the believers present. The imagery is of a physical temple (a meeting place between God and people) being built through a variety of skilled crafts. People are to sing, instruct, bring revelation, and practice the spectacular charismatic gifts of speaking in tongues and interpreting tongues. The "everyone" - or, as the ESV renders it, "each" - cannot mean that all people present must contribute; the later verses negate that (v29-33). Rather, it must mean that all present have a strong desire to contribute and not to be passive onlookers. Paul goes on to give guidelines to bring order in this context.

> *"The speakers therefore needed to be aware of what was going on in the meeting and to act accordingly."*

14:27

"If anyone speaks in a tongue, two - or at the most three - should speak, one at a time, and someone must interpret."

Paul has stated that speaking in tongues is one of the gifts that can be used in a public gathering, because when used maturely it is helpful in strengthening the church. Now he gives some specific instructions as to how that gift is to be used. There should be a sense of order and control: no more than two or three tongues in a given meeting, and each spoken one at a time. It was not to be chaotic but ordered and intelligible: someone was to interpret. The interpretation could be given by the speaker (v13) or by someone else, and it would always be addressed towards God (v2). The speakers therefore needed to be aware of what was going on in the meeting and to act accordingly. They were not to act subject to impulse but to behave in a way that was orderly and made use of the complementary gift of the interpretation of tongues (12v10).

14:28

"If there is no interpreter, the speaker should keep quiet in the church and speak to himself and to God."

From this instruction the question arises, how do you know if there is an interpreter before you speak the tongue? The person speaking the tongue may already have faith to give the interpretation themselves (v13). Or it could be that there is someone present who has a history of bringing interpretations (12v10), making it likely that they will again. But Paul may also be suggesting that the speaker should self-regulate: if they bring tongues over a number of meetings and there is never an interpretation, they should conclude to use their gift only as a private prayer language.

It is clear that Paul wants tongues to be used in the gatherings of the Corinthian church, that tongues are addresses to God, that they must be are interpreted, and that they strengthen the church. Who interprets the tongue is less important; that it is interpreted is vital. All should be done in an orderly manner so that both the tongue and its interpretation are heard by all and easily understood. For us at RFC, that means speaking slowly and using the microphone (so those who are hard of hearing are included).

"Who interprets the tongue is less important; that it is interpreted is vital."

14:29

"Two or three prophets should speak, and the others should weigh carefully what is said."

Just as Paul advises for the Corinthians' church meetings to include two or three tongues with interpretations, so are two or three people to prophesy. The gift of prophecy has been given for the common good (12v7,10), as has the gift of distinguishing between spirits. The apostle John wrote "do not believe every spirit, but test the spirits to see whether they are from God, for many false prophets have gone out into the world" 1 John 4v1. Whilst the context for John was false teaching, his advice does underscore the need for testing and weighing of prophecy.

Who does the 'weighing'; who are the 'others'? Most likely this refers not only to other people who have the gift of prophecy but includes the whole church: elders, deacons and everyone. They are not to despise prophecy but to test everything, and to hold fast to what is good (1 Thess 5v20). Even if the prophecy is good, the prophecy is still partial and there is room for error. It should be considered as incomplete rather than definitive. It is 'a seed of a promise' that needs to be carefully measured against the teaching of scripture before being nurtured (13v9).

14:30-31

"And if a revelation comes to someone who is sitting down, the first speaker should stop. For you can all prophesy in turn so that everyone may be instructed and encouraged."

Let's not forget that Paul's letter is written to a church with deep factions, who were actively using the charismatic gifts and particularly valued oratory gifts. Part of the challenge was getting them to recognise and honour the variety of gifts and contributions among their congregation. Paul's solution was deference to one another's gifting on the basis of love and mutual desire to build the church up. If a revelation came to someone who was sitting down listening, the first speaker should stop. How this was to be communicated is not written, but it is clear that the speaker should defer and stop. This simple rule guards against overly long contributions and also ensures that any speaker is in good standing (otherwise they can simply be shut down by someone else). This rule builds in honour and deference and produces an equilibrium for the two or three prophetic contributions. I suspect this is much easier to write than to practise!

14:32-33

"The spirits of prophets are subject to the control of prophets. For God is not a God of disorder but of peace."

We have here a glimpse of how Paul understands the function of the Spirit empowering His gifts in His people. It is a partnership and interaction: the Spirit gives the gift but does not take over, He does not compel the prophet to speak. The gift is empowered by the Spirit but remains subject to the speaker. Control is not lost, and no trance-like state is required. There is no sense of 'possession', as we saw in descriptions of oppressed demoniacs or those influenced by demons in the Gospels (Luke 9v39, Mark 5v15). The prophet's contribution is under their control; they are well able to stop mid-flow, and indeed must be willing to do so (see v30)! The reason for this is that the Spirit wants to be heard and understood when He speaks. For this to happen, a sense of order and peacefulness is required. Spontaneity is not a hallmark of spirituality. Genesis 1v1-2 states that in the beginning the earth was without form and void and the Spirit of God was hovering over the waters ready to do His work. The Spirit brought order out of chaos in the first few verses of the Bible, and He is still in that business.

> *"The Spirit brought order out of chaos in the first few verses of the Bible, and He is still in that business."*

14:33-34

> "As in all the congregations of the Lord's people, women should remain silent in the churches. They are not allowed to speak, but must be in submission, as the law says."

Most of us will find these verses jarring to read. They contain the difficult, loaded words of silence, submission and shame, and these directed at women. It is unexpected because it is contrary to the flow of the letter, earlier Paul says women can speak in church gatherings (11v5). It is emphatic 'as in all the churches of the saints'. So, what's going on? Scripture does not contradict itself so we must try to understand these verses in light of others. Joel 2v28-32 states that prophesy is the inheritance of all believers, regardless of gender. Acts 21v8-9 records that Paul visited the home of Philip the evangelist, who had four unmarried daughters who prophesied, presumably in church meetings. Priscilla was well-versed in Scripture and was helpful to Apollos (Acts 18v26). In Colossians 3v16 he urges them to corporately sing psalms, hymns and spiritual songs. So, Paul must have been responding to a specific situation such that the original readers would not have been confused by this apparent 'contradiction'. The immediate context is Paul's concern for orderly worship in general and the careful weighing of prophecy in particular (14v29). Paul's instruction for women to "remain silent, not speaking" must refer to "carefully weighing what is prophesied". This is not because women can't carefully weigh something, wisdom is personified as a woman in Proverbs 4v6-9. Rather it is because of the local customs and God's created order of headship (11v8-9), this is supported up by his reference to the Law (presumably Genesis 2v20-23).

14:35

> "If they want to inquire about something, they should ask their own husbands at home; for it is disgraceful for a woman to speak in the church."

Paul has already established that women (wives) can pray and prophesy in church (11v5) so long as it is done with an attitude of willingly yielding to God's created order. Paul affirms women's learning; they should learn. The worship meetings in Corinth were most likely organised along the lines of a synagogue, meaning men and woman would be segregated. It may well be that the women were discussing, weighing or questioning prophetic words amongst themselves and causing a disruption. Worse still, they may have been calling out and asking their husbands across the divide. What would be considered 'disgraceful' would be for a woman to publicly question the opinion of her husband (or the church elders) in weighing the prophecy. Paul is not suggesting it is unthinkable for a man to be wrong, rather, there was a expectation for how they were to be questioned. Most of the church, and unbelievers looking in (14v23), would have seen the expression of submission to her husband as a good thing and dishonouring your 'head' by questioning as disgraceful (11v6). As such, Paul tells the woman to ask and debate with her husband at home, not raise questions, or cause a disruption, in the church meeting. A wife is to honour her husband by directing questions to him, in so doing she is acting appropriately. Note that 'women' refers to married women, there was no practice of a single woman living alone. If you were an unmarried woman, you either lived with your family as a daughter or as a widower.

14:36

"Or did the word of God originate with you? Or are you the only people it has reached?"

Paul asks these two rhetorical questions to remind the Corinthians both that he taught them in their early days as a church, and that they don't exist alone (they are part of "the congregation of the saints" v33). They are not their own final authority: their authority is God's word, and Jesus was the word made flesh (John 1v14). Paul brought that 'word' to Corinth - as Acts 18 records - where he teamed up with Priscilla and Aquilla. Paul then moved on from Corinth to Ephesus, where he stayed for two years, resulting in all the Jews and Greeks who lived in the province of Asia (not to be confused with the continent of Asia) hearing the word of the Lord. As Paul writes to this beloved church, with all their factions and all their zeal, he calls them to order, to interdependence and to humility. They are the fruit of God's word and are part of a much bigger movement by God. How their meetings operate matters within the wider church; the congregations of the saints are connected not autonomous.

> *"He was given divine authority by Christ to lay a foundation as an expert builder."*

14:37

"If anyone thinks they are a prophet or otherwise gifted by the Spirit, let them acknowledge that what I am writing to you is the Lord's command."

Paul anticipates a few Corinthians disagreeing with his teachings and guidance on their worship meetings. He pre-emptively answers potential dissenters: "If you're spiritually mature you will agree with me", "If you think God speaks through you, you will agree that what I am saying is Jesus' command". He is affirming his divine authority on these matters; what he has written not merely his preferences. Those within the Corinthian church may have their preferred apostles (be that Apollos, Cephas, or Paul - 1v12) but he was teaching the Lord's command. Regardless of which apostle they look to, all the congregations of the saints, should follow this. Paul was called to be an apostle of Christ Jesus by the will of God (1v1). He was given divine authority by Christ to lay a foundation as an expert builder (3v10). He writes to them what Jesus commands.

14:38

> *"But if anyone ignores this, they will themselves be ignored."*

Paul is asserting his God-given authority as the father of the Corinthian church (1v1, 4v15). He writes that if anyone does not recognise or agree with what he has to say, their opinions and views should be disregarded. Given the many factions in the church (3v4) this would have been a provocative statement! Aspects of their meetings were doing more harm than good (11v17), and so needed to be addressed. The stakes were high. There are times in the life of a church that clear direction needs to be given and dissenters ignored.

Paul is anticipating pushback on his teaching, and stating it is the Lord's command only heightens the seriousness of what Paul is saying. Some things need to be fought for and held tightly to. Sometimes leaders need to assert God-given authority knowing it will squash and ignore the opinions of others. If people are prophetic or consider themselves spiritually gifted they will submit to God-ordained authority; otherwise they are to be ignored or not recognised.

> *"Structure in meetings can often squeeze out the charismatic gifts, or the use of charismatic gifts can squeeze out a sense of order. But Paul contends for both."*

14:39-40

> *"Therefore, my brothers and sisters, be eager to prophesy, and do not forbid speaking in tongues. But everything should be done in a fitting and orderly way."*

Paul sums up this section of his letter by urging the Corinthians of attitudes to foster, not by prescribing or proscribing activity. They are to follow the way of love and eagerly desire spiritual gifts, especially the gift of prophecy (14v1). They are to have a keen desire to strengthen, comfort and encourage one another. Tongues are not to be forbidden; they have their rightful place in corporate worship so long as they are interpreted. Church meetings are to demonstrate charismatic gifts; a supernatural component should hallmark their gatherings. But they should also have a clear sense of order and decency. Structure in meetings can often squeeze out the charismatic gifts, or the use of charismatic gifts can squeeze out a sense of order. But Paul contends for both. It is a tension to be held not a problem to be fixed. Both the spontaneous and the planned are to be embraced by believers and witnessed by unbelievers.

CHAPTER 15

15:1 | *"Now, brothers and sisters, I want to remind you of the gospel I preached to you, which you received and on which you have taken your stand."*

Paul now begins a new section of his letter, and his tone remains warm; he addresses the Corinthians as brothers and sisters, not mere followers. Paul was the first to proclaim Christ to them; now he reminds them of the old story of the cross and the central truth of resurrection. The Corinthians had received this message with faith, both Gentiles like Titus Justice and Jews like Crispus the synagogue ruler and his entire household (Acts 18v8). When Paul had first arrived in Corinth and preached the gospel he encountered serious opposition. During this turmoil Jesus spoke to Paul in a vision, urging him not to be afraid and to keep on speaking for He would save many people in that city (Acts 18v10). Many received the gospel message with faith and years later they were still standing in it. Paul's phrase 'taken your stand' conveys the sense of an active faith, one that endures, prevails and is visible to all. In their cosmopolitan and religiously diverse city, the Corinthian believers had received Christ and taken their stand for him.

> *"Paul's phrase 'taken your stand' conveys the sense of an active faith, one that endures, prevails and is visible to all."*

15:2 | *"By this gospel you are saved, if you hold firmly to the word I preached to you. Otherwise, you have believed in vain."*

The Gospel is something that needs to be proclaimed, believed in, and acted upon. It is not about a single moment or saying one prayer. It cannot be reduced to a kind of insurance policy, which is forgotten until the worst happens. The gospel demands we preach good news to ourselves and act upon it daily. Because we are saved, we continue to follow Christ. And because we continue to follow Christ, we are saved. The parable of the Sower teaches us to be good soil, to hear the word and understand it, to be those who go on to yield a crop 30, 60 or 100 times that which was sown (Matt 13v23). Holding firmly to the gospel demands tender hearts, hearts that are not choked by the cares of the world and the deceitfulness of riches. Paul does not want the Corinthians to have believed in vain. To be saved by the gospel is better understood as a continuous process: "I was saved, I am being saved, I will be saved".

15:3

> *"For what I received I passed on to you as of first importance: that Christ died for our sins according to the Scriptures,"*

The apostle Paul was unique in that he was not taught or given the gospel by another person; rather, he received it through a revelation from Jesus himself (Gal 1v12). This revelation spoke of a death for the benefit of others: Jesus was despised and rejected by men, smitten by God, 'pierced for our transgressions and crushed for our iniquities; upon him was the chastisement that brought us peace, and with his wounds we are healed' (Isa 53v3-5). Christ's death had a purpose. Jesus was the anointed one who was cut off; he is the city and sanctuary that was destroyed (Dan 9v26). Jesus was the Shepherd who was struck, and the sheep will be scattered (Zech 13v7). Scripture foretold Jesus' death for our sins, and Paul received this revelation directly from Christ. Now Paul has passed this message on as of first importance.

15:4

> *"that he was buried, that he was raised on the third day according to the Scriptures,"*

Buried and raised: this statement is so familiar to believers but nonetheless seems improbable and impossible to the natural mind. Without a doubt, Christ died. The soldiers who came to hasten his death had no need to break his legs (John 19v33). With Pilate's permission, Joseph of Arimathea took his body and placed it in a new tomb (John 19v38-42). Just as Jonah spent three days in the belly of a fish and was then spat out, so Jesus' body spent three days in the tomb before being spat out into resurrection life. Just as the fish wanted to consume and feed on Jonah but wasn't allowed, so death wanted to consume Jesus but couldn't. Just as the fish was commanded to release Jonah, so death was commanded to release Jesus' body. God's will could not be denied. Jesus himself predicted his resurrection in Matthew 12v40 "For just as Jonah was three days and three nights in the belly of the great fish, so will the Son of Man be three days and three nights in the heart of the earth". But the heart of the earth would not hold him. However improbable and impossible, Jesus rose from the heart of the earth and appeared to His own followers.

> *"However improbable and impossible, Jesus rose from the heart of the earth and appeared to His own followers."*

15:5
> *"and that he appeared to Cephas, and then to the Twelve."*

Simon, also called Peter or Cephas, was one of the first disciples (Matt 4v18). He was the first to confess "You are the Christ, the Son of the living God" (Matt 16v16). He was one of the three who were led up to a high mountain to witness Jesus' transfiguration. He was with Jesus in Gethsemane, and he fell asleep despite Christ's direct request to pray (Matt 26v41). He disowned Jesus three times (John 18v17, v25, v27). He was also one of the first disciples to know that Jesus had risen from the dead (Mark 16v7), and he was graciously reinstated by Him (John 21v15). The resurrected Christ had appeared to Peter and then to all of the twelve apostles. (Reference to the 12 reminds us that Judas was replaced: someone who had been with them the whole time had to take over the apostolic ministry. They cast lots and the lot fell to Matthias, so he was added to the eleven remaining disciples (Acts 1v26).) Peter probably visited the church in Corinth, and certainly had followers in the church (1 Cor 1v12).

> *"One day they will receive their own resurrection and will eternally bear witness to Christ's glorious life, death and resurrection."*

15:6
> *"After that, he appeared to more than five hundred of the brothers and sisters at the same time, most of whom are still living, though some have fallen asleep."*

Paul continues to build his case that Jesus was raised on the third day by referring to more than 500 witnesses. These people all saw Christ at the same time; presumably they were all gathered in one place, but they may not have been. At the time Paul was writing, most of these witnesses were still alive and able to give their account firsthand. We can safely assume this was during the period of 40 days "where he showed himself to these men and gave many convincing proofs that he was alive" (Acts 1v3). It is interesting that Paul has added that some have fallen asleep - a euphemism for dying. Falling asleep fits well in the language of faith and resurrection. Some of these witnesses had died and could no longer give testimony to Christ's resurrection. But one day they will receive their own resurrection and will eternally bear witness to Christ's glorious life, death and resurrection.

15:7 | *"Then he appeared to James, then to all the apostles,"*

Paul continues his list of people to whom the resurrected Christ appeared. James most likely refers to Jesus' half-brother; his others were Joseph, Simon and Judas (Matt 13v55). James became a key figure in the church at Jerusalem. When Peter was released from prison he sent a message to James (Acts 12v17). In Acts 15, James is an authority figure who makes the final judgement regarding Paul and Barnabas' mission to the Gentiles (Acts 15v21-31). Paul also refers to James in his letter to the Galatians, describing him as the Lord's brother, and as a pillar of the church alongside Cephas and John. So to refer to James as a witness to the resurrected Christ was a weighty claim. The other apostles Paul refers to presumably means those who were gifted by the ascended Christ (Eph 4v11) but didn't spend three years as his disciples, nor did they receive a direct vision of Jesus as Paul did.

> *"The Jew who was speaking murderous threats against the Master's servants finally met their Master"*

15:8 | *"and last of all he appeared to me also, as to one abnormally born."*

Paul was not one of the twelve who were with Jesus during his ministry, from John's baptism to his ascension (Acts 1v21). Paul first encountered Christ on the road to Damascus. The Jew who was speaking murderous threats against the Master's servants finally met their Master (Acts 9v5). The encounter with Jesus left Paul blind and he did not eat or drink anything for three days. In Damascus Paul had another vision, of a man called Ananias who would lay hands Paul to restore his sight (Acts 9v12). Sure enough, Ananias came, placed his hands on him and said "Brother Saul, the Lord Jesus, who appeared to you on the road as you were coming here, has sent me so that you may see again and be filled with the Holy Spirit" (Acts 9v17). Paul's sight was restored, he was baptised and he regained his strength. The great apostle who refers himself as abnormally born (of less standing in the eyes of others), has seen and bears witness to a resurrected Lord Jesus. He met him, on a road to Damascus. And the Lord later spoke to him in Corinth: "Do not be afraid, keep on speaking" (Acts 18v9-10).

15:9

"For I am the least of the apostles and do not even deserve to be called an apostle, because I persecuted the church of God."

We first hear of Saul in Acts 7v59 when Stephen was stoned to death. Saul stood nearby giving his approval and guarding the clothes of those who were killing Stephen (Acts 22v20). Saul zealously persecuted the followers of 'the Way' - that is, Jesus. His practice was to go from one synagogue to another, imprisoning and beating those who believed in Jesus, pursuing some to their death. His reputation preceded him because of the harm he had meted out to the saints in Jerusalem (Acts 9v13). Saul obtained letters from the Jewish council in Jerusalem to be given to their counterparts in Damascus, allowing him to take followers of Jesus back to Jerusalem for punishment (Acts 22v4-5). Paul had every reason to consider himself the least of all the apostles; he had ravaged the fledgling church, badly treated both men and women, and punished and tormented those who had put their trust in Jesus. The Corinthians celebrated apostles; Paul demotes himself because of his history, saying he is the least of the apostles.

15:10

"But by the grace of God I am what I am, and his grace to me was not without effect. No, I worked harder than all of them - yet not I, but the grace of God that was with me."

Despite Paul's heinous history he received unearned, unmerited, unending favour from God. Jesus met Paul, called him, forgave him, and accepted him. Jesus knew the worst of Paul yet still called him to be an apostle. And this grace had a profound impact on Paul. His response was gratitude, which led him to work harder than all of the other apostles. The reason he worked hard was not to qualify himself but because he was now qualified. God's grace was propelling him, motivating him and inspiring him. When a professional legalist declares they have worked harder than anyone else, you have to ask what was driving them. When Paul goes on to state it wasn't his own will or self-control but the grace of God, it changes the picture completely. The destination is the same - good works are done - but the journey is totally different.

"the reason he worked hard was not to qualify himself but because he was now qualified."

15:11

"Whether, then, it is I or they, this is what we preach, and this is what you believed."

Paul reminds the Corinthians of the message he preached to them: that Christ died for their sins, was buried, and rose from death on the third day (v3-4). It was this news that the apostles - including Paul - proclaimed, and it was this news that the Corinthians believed. This improbable news had many witnesses and could be verified. Paul cares little who gets the credit for proclaiming the gospel: he planted the seed, Apollos watered it, but God made it grow (3v6). Paul's fellow workers want to see a rich harvest from the field. They work to see God's temple of living stones built upon the foundation of Jesus (3v10). Paul desires kingdom advance. He has worked harder than all of the other apostles to proclaim Christ's resurrection. Paul wrote to the believers in Philippi in a similar vein: he had little concern over the motive of the speakers, the important thing was that Christ was preached in every city (Phil 1v18).

15:12

"But if it is preached that Christ has been raised from the dead, how can some of you say that there is no resurrection of the dead?"

Paul began this section by reminding the Corinthians of Christ's resurrection; now he directly challenges those amongst them who say there is no resurrection. In verses 3 and 4 he carefully built the ground of his argument: the Scriptures state the Messiah was to die (Isa 53v3-5, Dan 9v26, Zech 13v7) and would then be raised to life (Psa 16v10, Isa 53v10). The twelve disciples and 500 believers all saw the resurrected Jesus, as did James and Paul. Both scripture and the testimony of these 'senior' saints claim that Christ was raised from the dead. Paul now draws on the weight of this against the false teaching circulating in Corinth. Some of the believers had a wrong understanding of this key truth. The church in Corinth was divided, there was jealousy and quarrelling among them (3v1); it is little wonder that gospel truth got badly out of shape.

> *"Paul cares little who gets the credit for proclaiming the gospel: he planted the seed, Apollos watered it, but God made it grow."*

15:13-14

"If there is no resurrection of the dead, then not even Christ has been raised. And if Christ has not been raised, our preaching is useless and so is your faith."

Paul addresses directly those in Corinth who either denied the resurrection of the dead or else were confused about it. He has laid a foundation stating the truthfulness of Christ's resurrection; he now goes on to link Christ's resurrection to the resurrection of all believers. He urges the Corinthians to see and know that there is a seamless connection between Christ's resurrection in the past and the future resurrection of all who believe. For Paul, Christ was the prototype and the example of what is to come. He is saying that what happened to Jesus will happen to all those who have put their faith in Him. If Christ was not raised from the dead, neither will they be. And if Christ was not raised, then Paul's preaching and that of all the apostles is useless - such is the significance of the event. But Jesus was raised from the dead! Resurrection is the vindication of what happened on the cross.

> *"There is a seamless connection between Christ's resurrection in the past and the future resurrection of all who believe."*

15:15

"More than that, we are then found to be false witnesses about God, for we have testified about God that he raised Christ from the dead. But he did not raise him if in fact the dead are not raised."

Paul goes on to make a distinction between his mind and his spirit. His mind is the element of his being that enables him to think and to process the physical world around him. His spirit is the invisible, internal element of his being, the essence of who he is, the source of his emotion and character, and the part of him that is tuned into an awareness of God. Paul is saying that when he prays in a tongue his spirit is engaged but his intellect is not. He is uttering mysteries using his spirit that have not yet been disclosed to his mind (14v2). Remember the context of this statement: he is arguing that for the church to be built up they must be able to understand what is being said. Our minds need to be renewed in order for us to be transformed (Rom 12v2). Our minds need to be able to test what is spoken in order to discern the will of God and to know what is good. Speaking in tongues employs the spirit of a person but leaves their mind idle. But our minds need to be engaged if transformation is to occur.

15:16

> *"For if the dead are not raised, then Christ has not been raised either."*

Some of the teachers in the Corinthian church, or external influences on the church, had either severed or questioned the link between Christ's resurrection and that of believers. They argued there was no resurrection for those who followed Christ. Paul, however, restates his conviction of v11: if there is no resurrection of the dead, then not even Christ has been raised. Christ's resurrection and the resurrection of believers are bound together, just as day follows night. Christ has been raised, and there is a long list of witnesses (v5-8). So if Christ has been raised, so must those who have placed their faith in Him. Christ is the Head of a new humanity (v22). He is the first fruit, our prototype, the forerunner. Just as His death was credited as our death (Rom 6v8), so His resurrection assures our resurrection. If we have been united to him in His death, we will certainly also be united with him in his resurrection (Rom 6v5).

15:17

> *"And if Christ has not been raised, your faith is futile; you are still in your sins."*

If Jesus was not resurrected it would mean death still had a claim on him. By this I mean if Christ were not resurrected it would suggest His death was insufficient because his life was not good enough. It suggests his life and death did not meet the full penalty of sin and so atonement would not have been achieved. If this was the case, the Corinthians' faith would be futile as they would still have a debt of sin. God is holy and just, so sin needs to be accounted for. If Christ had not been raised it was because He was an inadequate offering.

Christ's resurrection is more than a historical fact with multiple witnesses. It was the public vindication and proof that his death was a sufficient and effective substitute for ours. Death could no more hold him than the fish could feed on Jonah. In Romans 4v25 Paul puts it like this: "He was delivered over to death for our sins and was raised to life for our justification". This new relationship was written in Christ's blood; his death became ours. Miraculously we are now fully identified with Jesus' death and resurrection.

> *"If Christ had not been raised it was because He was an inadequate offering."*

15:18

"Then those also who have fallen asleep in Christ are lost."

Paul uses the euphemism 'fallen asleep' not because the word 'death' might be insensitive to those who mourn but simply because it is closer to the truth. To fall asleep implies the expectation of later awakening. Paul also used the term 'fallen asleep' in 1 Thessalonians 4v15 to describe the resurrection: "we who are alive, who are left until the coming of the Lord, will not precede those who have fallen asleep". To fall asleep speaks of a temporary state of inactivity, which is a helpful metaphor for understanding death and resurrection.

Paul continues here the logic of the Corinthians' mistaken argument: if Christ has not been raised from the dead then Christians who have died are lost because death retains its claim and grip on both Christ and themselves. All hope of a joyful resurrection and eternal life is extinguished.

> *"If Christ has not been raised from the dead then Christians who have died are lost because death retains its claim and grip on both Christ and themselves."*

15:19

"If only for this life we have hope in Christ, we are of all people most to be pitied."

If Christ has not been raised then a life of faith in Him is futile: it is all for nothing. If this is the case then Christians should receive the greatest sympathy, because they have been cruelly deceived. Not only have they believed a lie but many of their contemporaries were martyred for it. Paul gave up his life as a zealous Pharisee and at the time of writing was hungry, thirsty, in rags, homeless and being brutally treated (4v11). He is to be especially pitied if if there is no resurrection. Yet Paul sees the Christian life as eternal: it stretches beyond death. If the benefit of faith in Christ is limited to this side of our death, then the gospel is emptied of meaningful hope. There would be no hope for a truly better day, a truly better body, a truly renewed heaven and earth. Christian hope is about the earth being renewed, an eternal Kingdom being established, and eternal life for believers in Christ. To remove that promise is to collapse the horizon, to remove motive, to snuff out true Christian hope.

15:20

> *"But Christ has indeed been raised from the dead, the firstfruits of those who have fallen asleep."*

Some of the Corinthians were teaching that there is no resurrection of the dead (v12). Paul countered this by reminding them of the gospel he preached to them (v1). This gospel included Christ being raised from the dead (v4), an event that was verified by hundreds of reliable witnesses (v6-8). Paul then affirmed that Christ was raised from the dead as the 'firstfruits' of a great resurrection harvest: He would be followed by those who died with faith in Christ. 'Firstfruits' is a familiar biblical term: Exodus 23v9 speaks of bringing the best of the 'firstfruits' of the harvest to the house of the Lord. 'Firstfruits' was a sample of what was to come, indicating the nature and quality of the crop. Christ is the firstfruits of the future resurrection harvest. His resurrection and the bodily form He took is a foretaste of the quality and nature of the believers' resurrection.

> *"'Firstfruits' was a sample of what was to come, indicating the nature and quality of the crop."*

15:21

> *"For since death came through a man, the resurrection of the dead comes also through a man."*

Paul now introduces the theological principle of two federal heads of humanity, by taking the readers back to Genesis 3. God saw Adam as the head of Eve. Adam was created first; Eve was created as a helper fit for him, and he named her (Gen 2v20-22). Adam remained silent while the Serpent deceived Eve. She yielded and he ate what was given to him by Eve (Gen 3v1-6). Both Adam and Eve were removed from the presence of God and forbidden to access the tree of life (Gen 3v22-24). Death entered into humanity through Adam's failure to exercise his God-given headship. Death entered humanity through Adam's sin. Adam is the default representative of all humanity; the only other representative, Jesus Christ, arrived thousands of years later. For Paul, humanity is divided between two heads of state: those who are in Adam's legacy, and those who have transferred into Christ's.

15:22

"For as in Adam all die, so in Christ all will be made alive."

All humanity, past, present and future, are divided into two tribes, each with their own federal head and family traits. Everyone starts in Adam, with his inherited sin passed down from generation to generation. When in Adam, the final outcome is death: both physical and, more importantly, an eternal, conscious, spiritual death. The other federal head is Christ. People transfer into His Kingdom by faith, and all receive the same outcome: a resurrection to eternal life, beyond the grave. Paul urges the Corinthians to reject any teaching that denies the resurrection of all followers of Christ. Since believers in Christ are no longer in the family line of Adam, the curse of death has no claim on them. God's judgement was meted on Christ. God has decided to attribute Christ's obedience and resurrection life to all who put their trust in Him.

15:23

"But each in turn: Christ, the firstfruits; then, when he comes, those who belong to him."

God's work of redemption to wholeness is progressive and orderly (14v33 and Genesis 1). The first-fruits are brought in before the whole harvest. Christ is the example, the representative and the pattern. His resurrection was both a vindication of God's plan of salvation and the pattern of ours. He was raised from the dead and given a renewed, imperishable body. He is now waiting to return - the hour and day of which are known only by the Father (Matt 24v36). But when He does finally come 'He will himself descend from heaven with a cry of command and the sound of the trumpet of God. The dead will rise first, then we who are alive, those who are left, will be caught up together with them in the clouds to meet the Lord in the air, and so we will always be with the Lord' (1 Thess 4v16-17). To say there is no resurrection of the dead is not gospel truth and should be strongly rejected (v12).

> *"His resurrection was both a vindication of God's plan of salvation and the pattern of ours."*

15:24

> *"Then the end will come, when he hands over the kingdom to God the Father after he has destroyed all dominion, authority and power."*

The 'end' Paul refers to is the end of this age, when all dominion, glory and God's Kingdom will be given over to Christ. At that point all people who have put their trust in Him will serve Him (Dan 7v14). At the end we will all see Christ as He truly is: far above all earthly rulers and authorities, with far greater power and dominion. His name will be above every name (Eph 1v21). At the end Jesus will be supreme and exalted by all - willingly or begrudgingly. As the federal head of the new humanity, Christ will hand over the kingdom to His heavenly Father. This act of giving will be the supreme demonstration that He has destroyed all dominions and authorities and powers. None will be able to challenge his status as the Kingdom giver. Jesus works to give glory, honour and the Kingdom to his Father.

15:25

> *"For he must reign until he has put all his enemies under his feet."*

Paul draws the Corinthians' attention to Jesus as the reigning Messianic King, seated at God's right hand. Jesus - their federal head - is the one spoken of in Psalm 110v1: "The Lord says to my Lord: 'Sit at my right hand, until I make your enemies your footstool'." God will subdue all His enemies, making all powers, dominions and authorities subject to Jesus' rule. Jesus is a reigning, victorious King with a growing Kingdom. He has been raised from the dead in a physical resurrection body. He was then exalted to the highest place of honour, seated at the right hand of God in the heavenly realms (Eph 1v20). Jesus' reign is robust and its outcome is guaranteed: all his enemies will be put under his feet. Whilst those in Adam languish in eternal death, those in Christ will be raised into his victory. They are made eternally alive because they are hidden in the One who destroys not only sin, Satan and death but overshadows every ruler, authority and power.

> *"This act of giving will be the supreme demonstration that He has destroyed all dominions and authorities and powers."*

15:26 | *"The last enemy to be destroyed is death."*

In Adam, death was the victor who held claim and dominion over all people. As a federal head, Adam was powerless concerning death. Yet Christ was victorious over death: it had no claim by which to hold him. All of Christ's enemies will be defeated. This includes all humans who rage against Him (the powers, authorities and dominions of humanity) as well as in, Satan (including his demons) and death. The last of the enemies to be destroyed is death; in our post-resurrection present, death is defeated but not yet destroyed. Jesus has abolished death and brought life and immortality (2 Tim 1v10). Through Christ's death he will destroy the one who has the power of death - that is, the devil - and deliver all those who were subject to lifelong slavery through fear of death (Heb 2v14-15). The moment where death is destroyed is depicted in Revelations 20v14: "Death and Hades were thrown into the lake of fire". Revelations 21v4 records "He will wipe away every tear from their eyes, and death shall be no more".

> *"The Father glorifies the Son so that the Son may glorify the Father."*

15:27 | *"For he 'has put everything under his feet.' Now when it says that 'everything' has been put under him, it is clear that this does not include God himself, who put everything under Christ."*

We would do well to remember that this section of the letter started with Paul pointing out the Corinthians' confusion around resurrection (v12). This led Paul to link their resurrection with Christ's resurrection, to point to the supremacy of Christ over Adam, and finally to remind them that Christ is exalted over all things. God raised Christ from the dead and made all created things to be subject to him - clearly, 'all created things' does not include God the creator! Rather, Jesus will hand all things over to God the Father (v24). Paul is ensuring that there is no confusion regarding how Father and Son relate to one another. The Father sends the Son (John 3v16); the Son is obedient to the Father (Luke 22v42). The Father puts all things under Christ's feet and exalts him to his right hand (Eph 1v20). The Father glorifies the Son so that the Son may glorify the Father (John 17v1). It is a beautiful relationship of mutual honouring and giving.

15:28

"When he has done this, then the Son himself will be made subject to him who put everything under him, so that God may be all in all."

Here, Paul underlines the relationship between the eternal Father and Son. The Bible clearly and repeatedly affirms that there is one God (Deut 6v4) who is also three persons (Matt 28v19). The Bible also teaches that there is an established order: Father, Son and Spirit work in unity with one will. Jesus is equal to the Father in his divinity; He tells us "I and the Father are one" (John 10v30). And Jesus submits Himself to the Father: "The Son can do nothing of his own accord, but only what he sees the Father doing" (John 5v19). This submission was not just for Jesus' brief time on earth as God incarnate, but has continued and will continue eternally. God the Father will continually remain the head of Jesus and supreme over all creation including the renewed creation, never to be deposed.

> *"The Bible also teaches that there is an established order: Father, Son and Spirit work in unity with one will."*

15:29

"Now if there is no resurrection, what will those do who are baptised for the dead? If the dead are not raised at all, why are people baptised for them?"

The church in Corinth was influenced by all sorts of strange teaching. Some people were proud that their new-found freedom allowed a man to have sex with his father's wife (5v1), whilst others stopped having sex with their spouse (7v5). There were also some within the church who were being baptised on behalf of dead believers. Paul uses this practice of baptism for the dead to show that some Corinthians believers are very confident in the resurrection. He argues that their practice of 'baptism for the dead' makes no sense and is futile if there is no resurrection. It is important to note that in no other passage is baptism for the dead mentioned. Paul is not affirming it as appropriate, he is simply reporting that it was a practice amongst them. Scripture is consistent in its teaching that salvation comes through a personal confession of faith in Christ, not through the act of baptism, nor through baptism by proxy.

15:30 | "And as for us, why do we endanger ourselves every hour?"

Paul now moves the spotlight off the Corinthians and onto his own suffering for the gospel. Because of his faith in Christ and the resurrection he has endured many dangers: from rivers, from robbers, from his own people, from false brothers, from Gentiles, in the city, in the wilderness, and at sea. He has also endured many hardships and much toil (2 Cor 11v26-27). If there is no resurrection, Paul is to be pitied more than all men because all of this would have been in vain. Even at the time of writing (he is with Sosthenes in Ephesus) he considers himself in danger from those who oppose the gospel: Ephesus erupted into a riot and Paul's companions feared for his life (Acts 19v30). Sosthenes was beaten in Corinth by the Jews (Acts 18v17). Paul's faith in Christ and His resurrection would continually lead him into hardship and danger.

15:31 | "I face death every day—yes, just as surely as I boast about you in Christ Jesus our Lord."

Here Paul picks up on Jesus' teaching in Luke 9v23: "If anyone would come after me, let him deny himself and take up his cross daily and follow me". Paul dies to his own desires and preferences on a daily basis because of his calling to follow Jesus. He daily faces brutal treatment, is hungry and thirsty, endures opposition and homelessness. He works hard with his own hands yet is cursed and considered the scum of the earth (4v11-13). But he considers that a price worth paying given his love for the saints. He loves the Corinthians as he loves the church in Thessalonica: they are his hope and joy, they are his crown of boasting before the Lord Jesus (1 Thess 2v19). Just as a father delights in his children, so Paul delights in the Corinthians. As a good father makes personal sacrifices and denies himself to provide for his children, so does Paul for his descendants in the faith. He spends himself for them, that they may hold fast to what he passed on to them: that "Christ died and was raised on the third day according to Scripture" (v3).

> "Paul's faith in Christ and His resurrection would continually lead him into hardship and danger."

15:32

> *"If I fought wild beasts in Ephesus with no more than human hopes, what have I gained? If the dead are not raised, 'Let us eat and drink, for tomorrow we die.'"*

Although there is no account in the book of Acts of Paul literally fighting with beasts, we have no reason to assume it did not happen. Paul begins his second letter to the church in Corinth stating that he suffered many hardships, to the point of despair, and was delivered from deadly perils (2 Cor 1v8). One of these ordeals was to face wild beasts because of his faith in Christ and his unwillingness to renounce him. For Paul, Christ's resurrection and the promise of his own means that he could lose his life and yet consider that gain (Phil 1v21). His willingness to endure the anguish and fear of being torn apart as a spectacle for others' entertainment only makes sense if the dead in Christ are raised. What we think and believe should be shaping how we live and how we die; Paul's overarching narrative and reason for writing is to remind the Corinthians of their share in Christ's resurrection.

15:33

> *"Do not be misled: 'Bad company corrupts good character.'"*

The English proverb "one bad apple spoils the barrel" expresses the same sentiment as Paul quotes here. Who the Corinthian believers spend time with will have an impact on them - for good or bad. Paul urges them to consider who is influencing them. There were many influences on and within their church: some for good, others for trouble (11v19). Paul wants the Corinthians to discern which of their fellow believers they should be open to. It is worth noting that the principle he is highlighting is that bad companions corrupt, not that good company redeems. Hanging out with bad company will, most likely, ruin good morals. Rarely will someone's good character transform the morals of those around them; that work is reserved for God. Believers are to be mindful of who is influencing them and be prepared to make changes where necessary. The spiritual person judges all things (2v15). We do well to be mindful of who we allow to influence us - though we need not withdraw from society.

> *"Paul's overarching narrative and reason for writing is to remind the Corinthians of their share in Christ's resurrection."*

15:34

"Come back to your senses as you ought, and stop sinning; for there are some who are ignorant of God—I say this to your shame."

Paul sharply concludes this section of his letter by telling the Corinthian believers to sober up and stop sinning! Whilst this may seem like an overreaction, some in the church had drifted into significant doctrinal error by saying there was no resurrection of the dead. This had to be emphatically countered. Another translation renders Paul's statement "Wake up from your drunken stupor, as is right, and do not go on sinning" (ESV). He dismisses their thinking as alcohol-fuelled nonsense, spoken by sinful and foolish people, who have long since been in an alcohol induced slumber! The phrase "some who are ignorant of God" refers either to the unbelievers in their meetings (14v23) or to the faction who deny the resurrection, who are very far from being "wise in Christ" as they claim in 4v10. Paul doesn't want seekers or less established believers to be confused and stumble.

> ## *"Ezekiel's vision reminds us that God is well able to bring new life to old bones."*

15:35

"But someone will ask, 'How are the dead raised? With what kind of body will they come?'"

Not only did some of the Corinthians say there was no resurrection (15v12) at all, others were clearly confused as to the nature of the resurrected body. Paul begins a new section of his letter by affirming that God will change their finite mortal bodies into eternal, immortal bodies. This will take some explanation. The ESV study Bible refers to Ezekiel's vision of the valley of dry bones and the Lord asking "can these bones live?". Ezekiel watches as bones connect to bone, sinews, flesh and skin then finally gain breath all at God's command. This was a vision of new life through the Spirit, prefiguring the giving of resurrection life and pointing forward to God raising His people from the grave (Eze 37v12-13). Whether Paul himself had this reference in mind is not clear, but without a doubt Ezekiel's vision reminds us that God is well able to bring new life to old bones.

15:36
> *"How foolish! What you sow does not come to life unless it dies."*

Although Corinth was a seaport the locals would still have understood this agricultural illustration. They knew that seed needed to be thrown on the ground and covered in earth in order for it to be transformed into something new. Jesus used this same illustration in John 12v24: "unless a grain of wheat falls into the earth and dies, it remains alone; but if it dies, it bears much fruit". Unless a seed is thrown to the ground and 'dies' (that is, is buried), no transformation will take place. The death of the seed must happen first; it must be buried in order to begin its new life. Some in Corinth thought that people who have been buried cannot be raised from the dead, that the body is abandoned by God and left to rot in the grave eternally. For Paul this is foolish: he argues that the body is sown in order for it to be renewed and transformed, much like seeds planted into the ground. Just as there is a direct link between the seed sown and the plant that grows, so it is with the body that is sown and the body that is raised.

15:37
> *"That he was buried, that he was raised on the third day according to the Scriptures."*

Paul uses a principle from nature to explain resurrection: you do not plant the mature crop, you just plant seeds. In the faithfulness and benevolence of God, the seed grows and is transformed into a stalk of wheat. A seed of grain is sown, and from it comes a stalk 50cm tall. This farming principal helps us to understand the resurrection - and much of life. Churches get started by a few Christ-centred people who scatter and plant themselves as Gospel seed. From these few who bury themselves in a local setting, thriving Christ-centred communities are established. This is Corinth's story. Paul proclaimed Christ in the synagogue, then in the house of Titius Justus, with fear and trembling and unimpressive speech (2v1-2). And God caused a vibrant church of Jews and Greeks, the rich and poor, the influential and slaves to grow (Acts 18v8, 11v22, 1v26, 12v13).

> *"From these few who bury themselves in a local setting, thriving Christ-centred communities are established."*

15:38 | *"But God gives it a body as he has determined, and to each kind of seed he gives its own body."*

God is the designer, agent and driving force of all life and growth. He has determined all things, including the shape and form of the vegetation of the land, "every seed-bearing plant and tree on the land that bears fruit with seed in it, according to their various kinds" (Gen 1v11). And God saw that it was good. He also sets limits so that each kind of seed can only produce one kind of plant (let's bypass the debate about genetically modified crops!). Paul is reminding the Corinthians of the created order and the activity of God in the world around them. Whatever they sow does not come to life except by God's decree; even the final form is determined by God through the genetic blueprint He placed in the seeds. Seeds fall to the ground, plants grow: God's creation continues in its order and purpose.

> ## *"God is the designer, agent and driving force of all life and growth."*

15:39 | *"Not all flesh is the same: People have one kind of flesh, animals have another, birds another and fish another."*

God has designed and ordered His creation such that all living and breathing things are different in 'flesh'. Genesis records that God made a distinction between vegetation - that can make its own food but cannot move around - and the animals, which can move around but can't make their own food. Amazing. Day five saw God create living creatures designed to make the waters teem with life and birds to fly above the earth across the expanse of sky (Gen 1v20-21). Day six saw the creation of land-based animals: livestock, wild animals and creatures that move along the ground (Gen 1v25). Day six also saw the pinnacle of creation: "God created man in his own image, in the image of God he created him, male and female he created them" (Gen 1v27). All of these living beings took different forms based on the decisions of a creative and benevolent God.

15:40

"There are also heavenly bodies and there are earthly bodies; but the splendour of the heavenly bodies is one kind, and the splendour of the earthly bodies is another."

Paul continues his illustration by pointing to heavenly and terrestrial 'bodies'. On the second day of creation God said "Let there be an expanse between waters to separate waters from waters", and the sky was made. Water vapour and an atmosphere were created. On day three God gathered the water under the sky to one place, and dry ground appeared: land and seas were created (Gen 1v9). The splendour of the sky at sunset, or daybreak, or after a thunderstorm, or when filled with vast cumulus clouds (the puffy cotton wool types) can be stunning. Or consider the splendour of crashing waves, or majestic mountain ranges, or lush forests, or green meadows with summer flowers, or the lakes and oceans. Even the frozen glaciers and polar ice-caps have a glory and splendour given them by a wise and loving God.

> *"Even the frozen glaciers and polar ice-caps have a glory and splendour given them by a wise and loving God."*

15:8

"The sun has one kind of splendour, the moon another and the stars another; and star differs from star in splendour."

Paul now directs his audience's attention to God's work of creating the celestial bodies on day four: the greater light to rule the day and the lesser light to rule the night (Gen 1v16). The sun is a huge ball of hot gas about 109 times bigger than earth, 330,000 times the mass of our planet, meaning it produces enough gravity to be the centre of our solar system. The moon is the largest satellite in our solar system, although because of its distance, orbit and position on occasions it can almost perfectly eclipse the sun. It affects the tides and the length of the day. The moon's surface is dark but reflects light from the sun. Each heavenly body has its own kind of splendour. It is part of a solar system, a galaxy and the created universe. There is one star in our solar system (which we call the sun), 100 billion stars in our galaxy (which we call the Milky Way), and millions upon millions of galaxies in the universe. That is a lot of differing splendour!

15:42

"So will it be with the resurrection of the dead. The body that is sown is perishable, it is raised imperishable;"

Just as God created all terrestrial and celestial bodies but assigned differing kinds and amounts of splendour, so will it be with the resurrection of the dead. A seed is sown and becomes a body with differing splendour. The splendour of the plant is different from - and arguably greater than - that of the seed. Both are created 'good' but one is brighter in glory, just as the sun, moon and stars differ in splendour, grandeur and magnificence. So too the resurrection body will have more magnificent features and qualities when compared to the mortal body. The body that is sown (that dies) is perishable, and prone to sickness and decay. By contrast the body that is raised is imperishable: it is enduring, everlasting, ageless and immortal. The resurrection body has a much greater splendour because, if nothing else, it is eternal in nature.

15:43

"it is sown in dishonour, it is raised in glory; it is sown in weakness, it is raised in power;"

The human body has been corrupted by both inherited and volitional sin (that is, sin by choice). The human body ages and inevitably decays. Its dishonour is displayed in its degradation; that which was designed by God and declared good is now disgraced and debased by sin's insidious and pervasive effect. This body is buried in all its weakness. But these lowly bodies will one day be transformed to be like Jesus' glorious body. his will be done by the power that enables Him to subject all things to himself (Phil 3v21). The grave can not resist such power and so must give up the dead. When Christ returns, those who placed their trust in him will also appear with Him in glory (Col 3v4). That which was laid to rest in weakness and dishonour will be transformed. No longer will those made in the image of God have that glory tainted, instead they will reflect a measure of the divine splendour of God!

> *"No longer will those made in the image of God have that glory tainted, instead they will reflect a measure of the divine splendour of God!"*

15:44

"it is sown a natural body, it is raised a spiritual body. If there is a natural body, there is also a spiritual body."

Paul uses the existence of the natural body to demand the existence of a spiritual body. They are a linked pair, much like day follows night. The 'natural body' refers to the skin and bones the Corinthians currently know as their bodies. But because of the sin of their federal head Adam, this body is temporary and doomed to perish. The 'spiritual body' refers to the body they are to receive at the resurrection. This body is raised by the Spirit's power and is eternal in nature. Paul sees death as the great divide of the two bodies that believers are fitted with. Before death, believers (and unbelievers) have a natural body, a ruin destined to be sown into death. After death, when Christ returns, believers will receive a glorious spiritual body that will be unhindered by sin, sickness or any other form of decay. The spiritual body is material (it is not ethereal or intangible) and an order of magnitude greater and more magnificent than the natural body.

15:45

"So it is written: 'The first man Adam became a living being'; the last Adam, a life-giving spirit."

Paul is referring here to the account in Genesis when God formed Adam from the dust of the ground and breathed into his nostrils the breath of life. Adam became a living creature with a soul - his spirit (Gen 2v7). Adam, our federal head, was created from dust and received life from God. From Adam we have received a perishable, flawed, dishonoured and weak natural body. This temporary body will be sown to the grave. The first Adam received life from God, but the 'last Adam' gives life from God. Christ is the second federal head, of all those who place their trust in Him. And He is a giver. At the resurrection, He will give a body to all those who follow Him. That body will be imperishable, glorious and empowered by the Spirit of God. Christ, the last Adam, gives eternal life, raising from the grave: "For as the Father raises the dead and gives life, so also the Son gives life to whom he will" (John 5v21).

> "The first Adam received life from God, but the 'last Adam' gives life from God."

15:46

"The spiritual did not come first, but the natural, and after that the spiritual."

There is order to God's purpose and plans: first the natural body, then the spiritual body. In his second letter Paul describes our earthly bodies using the image of a tent that will be destroyed and replaced by a building from God (2 Cor 5v1). Clearly a building is far greater than a tent. So, in the purposes of God, humankind was created in God's image and given a natural, earthly body that will be sown into the ground. But after that, when Christ returns, those bodies will be resurrected and renewed. There is order and progression in God's plans: the natural precedes the spiritual, the temporary precedes the eternal, the marred precedes the glorious. The body that ages, decays and is sown to dust will be renewed as a body that is eternal, empowered and raised for glory. The latter is far greater than the former.

> *"There is order and progression in God's plans: the natural precedes the spiritual, the temporary precedes the eternal, the marred precedes the glorious."*

15:47

"The first man was of the dust of the earth; the second man is of heaven."

The contrast between the two federal heads of humanity could not be more stark. The first man, Adam, was created out of the dust from the ground. He needed life breathed into him: he was a recipient, a created being who needed to be sustained by God. The second man, Jesus, is of heaven. He was and is eternally existent as the second person of the Godhead. He was not created, but took on flesh - was incarnated - when He stepped into time (John 1v14). He always has and always is sustaining all things by his powerful word (Heb 1v3). By Him all things were created, and all things were created for him (Col 31v16-18). The first man had dominion over a garden; the second man has supremacy in all things. The first man was created; the second man was the Creator. The first man was given dignity, value and purpose by God; the second man was the exact representation of the 'being' of God and His glory (Heb 1v3). The first is a son of God; the second is God's Son (John 3v16). The contrast between the man of dust and the man of heaven could not be greater.

15:48

> *"As was the earthly man, so are those who are of the earth; and as is the heavenly man, so also are those who are of heaven."*

Here Paul is hammering home the supremacy of Christ. Adam, the man of dust, was given everything he needed, including an instruction: he must not eat from the tree in the middle of the garden (Gen 3v3). But he chose disobedience. He wanted to be like God, who knew, to gain a knowledge he had been denied (Gen 3v5-6). Adam abdicated his God-given responsibility and allowed himself to be led astray. As it was with Adam, the man of dust, so it is with all those who are 'in' him; they choose disobedience and abdication because they want to be like God. They want to be their own gods. But the man of heaven - Jesus, the second Adam - chose obedience and responsibility to God when He was tempted by the same deceiver. The man of heaven passed his test in the desert: he held onto and submitted to God's word. The same is true of those who are of heaven: they pursue obedience to God, submitting themselves to the Bible's teaching.

15:49

> *"And just as we have borne the image of the earthly man, so shall we bear the image of the heavenly man."*

Paul now refers to Adam as 'the earthly man'. Just as his son Seth was born in the image and likeness of his father, Adam (Gen 5v3), so too are all of humanity. It is not that we physically resemble him, but that we have inherited the family trait of disobedience to God. Adam has passed that on to all of humanity. We are all 'Seths' in that we are all like his father; we share in all his glory, disobedience and weakness. But Paul reminds the Corinthians that one day they will be free from their likeness to the earthly man: their bodies will be transformed in the renewed heaven and earth. God predetermined that His chosen people would become like the man from heaven, Jesus: "For those whom God foreknew, He also predestined to be confirmed to the image of His Son, in order that He might be the firstborn among many brothers" (Rom 8v29). This happens by proxy during our time on earth but is fulfilled in our resurrection bodies. Once we resembled Adam; soon we shall resemble Jesus. We will bear his likeness!

> *"Once we resembled Adam; soon we shall resemble Jesus. We will bear his likeness!"*

15:50

"I declare to you, brothers and sisters, that flesh and blood cannot inherit the kingdom of God, nor does the perishable inherit the imperishable."

Paul uses the term 'flesh and blood' here to refer to the natural, earthly, 'dust of the ground' bodies that all people inherited from Adam. Whilst this creation was originally declared "good" by God (Gen 2v31), all have been corrupted by sin and are therefore destined to return to the dust (Gen 3v19). This marred, perishable body has no claim on nor can be part of the Kingdom of God. The entitlement to receive God's Kingdom and eternal life was forfeited by the rebellion in Eden. The inheritance passed on to Adam's descendants is exclusion from both the presence of God and access to the tree of life. Adam was driven out and banished from the garden of Eden; Cherubim and a flaming sword were stationed to guard the tree of life and deny Adam access (Gen 3v22-24). So now all flesh and blood will perish and return to the dust.

> *"All believers will receive from Christ a glorious, immortal and imperishable body - much like His."*

15:51

"Listen, I tell you a mystery: We will not all sleep, but we will all be changed-"

When Paul refers here to 'a mystery' he means something that hasn't yet been disclosed rather than something that is unknowable. Much of Paul's ministry is revealing truths from scripture that have remained hidden (Eph 3v1-6). Paul is going to explain the mystery that not everyone will die, but all who put their trust in Christ will be transformed. In this context Paul's reference to 'sleep' means death. Christ will return at a point in the future, at a time only known by the Father (Matt 24v36). When Jesus returns the dead will rise first, then those who are still alive will be caught up together with them in the clouds to meet the Lord in the air (1 Thess 4v16-17). During this great event all believers will receive their renewed bodies, which will be totally transformed. Regardless of whether we are alive or dead when He returns, we shall be changed. All believers will receive from Christ a glorious, immortal and imperishable body - much like His.

15:52

"in a flash, in the twinkling of an eye, at the last trumpet. For the trumpet will sound, the dead will be raised imperishable, and we will be changed."

Trumpets were often used as a means of communication in the ancient world. We read in Numbers 10 that God commands special trumpets to be sounded to gather the tribes, in preparation for meeting with God at the tent of meeting. Trumpets were also used to sound the command to pack up their camp and continue the daily advance into the Promised Land. And the prophet Isaiah speaks of a great trumpet being blown, and those who were lost or driven out of their inherited land would come and worship the Lord on the holy mountain at Jerusalem (Isa 27v13). In his statement Paul most likely has in mind this trumpet calling God's people to get ready for the last great exodus into the true dwelling place of the chosen people. Jesus said that the dead will rise to the resurrection life (John 5v26): their bodies will be raised imperishable, forever changed. Both the dead and the living will be transformed in the twinkling of an eye. It will be instantaneous, not a painful, drawn out affair. The old body that was sown into the dust will be changed without any perceptible duration of time.

> *"The second Adam's obedience made a way for the tent of our bodies to be replaced by a building from God, an eternal house in heaven, that is not built by human hands."*

15:53

"For the perishable must clothe itself with the imperishable, and the mortal with immortality."

Paul introduces the imperative "must" to mean that there is an urgency, a necessity to the transformation that will happen to the perishable and mortal body. He expands on this idea in a subsequent letter to the Corinthian believers, where he speaks of them groaning and longing to put on their heavenly dwellings, so that what is mortal may be swallowed up by life (2 Cor 5v2). God has prepared this very thing, and has given His Spirit as a guarantee. Humankind was never designed to die; death is a violation of the original design! The sin of the first Adam had a devastating effect: it introduced decay and physical death. But the obedience of the second Adam made a way for the perishable to be clothed with the imperishable, the mortal with immortality. The second Adam's obedience made a way for the tent of our bodies to be replaced by a building from God, an eternal house in heaven, that is not built by human hands (2 Cor 5v1).

15:54

"When the perishable has been clothed with the imperishable, and the mortal with immortality, then the saying that is written will come true: 'Death has been swallowed up in victory.'"

The phrase Paul quotes refers to Isaiah 25v6-8 where the prophet depicts the Lord of hosts on His mountain setting out a feast of rich foods and well-aged wine for His people. As he gathers them to feast at His table He will publicly swallow up death: He will consume it, and wipe away the tears from their faces. On His holy mountain, He will destroy the shroud of death that enfolds all people; the grave clothes and all disgrace will finally be removed. This prophetic picture will be fulfilled at Christ's second coming; the trumpet will sound and Christ shall return as victorious Champion and King. He is the One who has resoundingly defeated death; death has lost its claim on the mortal and perishable bodies that trusted in Christ. On that day, His people will say "Surely this is our God; we trusted him and he saved us. This is the LORD, we trusted him; let us rejoice and be glad in his salvation" (Isa 25v9).

15:55

"Where, O death, is your victory? Where, O death, is your sting?"

Paul refers here to Hosea 13v14; he replaces the word 'plagues' with 'victory' but the sentiment is the same. In Hosea's context, Ephraim (Israel) was rejecting God, the only power that could save them from death and eternal damnation. Because of Ephraim's rebellion against God, death's victory is complete: its sting has been neutralised. Paul refers to this because it has been changed for all who put their trust in Jesus, the second Adam. In Hosea's time, God's people rejected the only one who could save them from death's plagues and neutralise the sting of death's destruction. For the Corinthians, the 'man from heaven' is their strong deliverer: He is the One who has overcome death, He is the firstfruits of those who have died (v20). If He is their champion, then death has no lasting victory! Rather, Jesus snatches victory from death. The resurrection at Christ's return removes death's sting!

> *"He is the One who has resoundingly defeated death; death has lost its claim on the mortal and perishable bodies that trusted in Christ."*

15:56

> *"The sting of death is sin, and the power of sin is the law."*

The "sting" is the agent through which something toxic is delivered, it is the means by which enters the system. In Paul's letter to the church in Rome he wrote that "sin entered the world through one man, and death came through sin" (Rom 5v12). Adam was commanded by God to not to eat fruit from the tree in the middle of the garden. But he did. This disobedience to God (that is, sin) opened the way for death to wreak havoc on God's good creation. Death is 'unnatural' for mankind and is the inevitable and unavoidable consequence of sin. God wrote this consequence into the moral law evident in the fabric of creation (Rom 1v19). It is most clearly defined in the Mosaic Law which reveals the moral shortfall in our individual lives. Humanity cannot shrug off sin: God's law will call us to account. Every wagging tongue trying to defend itself will be silenced. Through the law we become conscious of sin (Rom 3v20). Death in itself is not a problem to God - he did, after all, raise Jesus out of it. But Sin is a problem. And the law exposes our sin.

15:57

> *"But thanks be to God! He gives us the victory through our Lord Jesus Christ."*

The victory over sin that we could not secure for ourselves has been given to us by the second Adam. Death could not defeat him. His resurrection was the proof of his victory and supremacy. Death could not hold him, and it will not hold us, for Christ's victory is now our victory. Now, in all things - not least death - we are made more than conquerors through Him who loved us (Rom 8v37). John wrote that everyone who has been born of God overcomes the world (1 John 5v4). The wonder is always that the Father shares His Son's victory so liberally with those who were disobedient. The victory that only the man from Heaven could secure is graciously given and credited to all who put their faith in Him. By faith in Jesus, they can join in His victory parade. They will be fitted with a resurrection body like the resurrected victorious King's. Thanks be to God! They, and we, shall bear the likeness of the man from Heaven. Hallelujah!

> *"Death in itself is not a problem to God - he did, after all, raise Jesus out of it. But Sin is a problem. And the law exposes our sin."*

15:58

"Therefore, my dear brothers and sisters, stand firm. Let nothing move you. Always give yourselves fully to the work of the Lord, because you know that your labor in the Lord is not in vain."

Paul concludes this lengthy section on the resurrection with a practical application: because Christ was raised from the dead, because the Corinthian believers will be raised from the dead, because they will be clothed with the imperishable, and because death has lost its sting, they are to stand firm! Paul urges them to be steadfast and immovable in their faith, and to abound in good works. They are not to be tossed to and fro by waves and winds of fear, worries and setbacks. They must stand firm against false teaching, human cunning and deceitful scheming (Eph 4v14). They are to give themselves fully to the work of the Lord. They are to believe in Jesus (John 6v29) and to go and make disciples (Matt 28v19). They are to plant and water knowing that each will receive wages according to his labour (3v8). No good act that is done in the name of Jesus will be overlooked or unrewarded in the age to come - not even a "cup of cold water" given (Matt 10v42).

> *"Paul urges them to be steadfast and immovable in their faith, and to abound in good works."*

CHAPTER 16

16:1
"Now about the collection for the Lord's people: do what I told the Galatian churches to do."

The area of Galatia was located in what we now call Turkey. Paul travelled through there on each of his great missionary journeys (Acts 14v1, 16v2, 18v23). As he passed through he preached the gospel and helped to establish a church. He would then revisit that church or send them letters to answer their questions or to bring direction. These epistles - like the one we are studying - included personal greetings as well as instructions on church doctrine and practice. The verse above concerns the provision for the poor in God's household. This specific collection is most likely for those in the Jerusalem church (Acts 24v17). When Agabus visited Antioch he prophesied a severe famine, and the disciples there were compelled to provide for their brothers and sisters living in Jerusalem (Acts 11v29). Provision for the poor was always at the heart of apostolic ministry: the apostles asked Paul to continue to remember the poor, the very thing he was eager to do (Gal 2v10); Romans 15v25-26 records Paul's ongoing concern for and service to the poor amongst the saints.

> *"He is not asking them to come up with a one-off gift but requiring them to form an ongoing, intentional habit."*

16:2
"On the first day of every week, each one of you should set aside a sum of money in keeping with your income, saving it up, so that when I come no collections will have to be made."

Here we have a glimpse of Paul's faith in action: he gives practical instruction about providing for the poor. He advises that every week, each of the Corinthian believers should set aside a sum of money for the upcoming collection. He is not asking them to come up with a one-off gift but requiring them to form an ongoing, intentional habit. The sum should be in accordance with their income, thereby ensuring both rich and poor are involved. From those who have been given much, much will be expected (Luke 12v48). It would have taken time for Paul to visit, so the sum of money they set aside would grow over the weeks. They would be required to exercise discipline not to dip into it. This would require both faith and planning, and would keep the needs of the poor prominent in the minds and lives of the Corinthian believers. Watching the stacks of coins grow would, no doubt, test their motives and faith in God to meet their own needs.

16:3

"Then, when I arrive, I will give letters of introduction to the men you approve and send them with your gift to Jerusalem."

Paul anticipates that he will visit the Corinthians again, and that when he does the money will be collected and dispatched to the saints in Jerusalem. It is worth noting that Paul is doing three things here. Firstly, he is sending the appointed Corinthian men as 'delegates' of his apostolic ministry, fulfilling the charge his fellow apostles in Jerusalem gave him to 'continue to remember the poor' (Gal 2v10). Secondly, he is wisely sending them as approved 'stewards' of the Corinthians' offering. This prevents any criticism of the way this gift is administered (2 Cor 8v20). Thirdly, he is sending them as 'brothers'. The church in Corinth are fellow heirs of Christ and therefore part of the same household as the church in Jerusalem. This is a church giving to another church, which fosters a joyful sense of togetherness. This is not a centralised donation to a generic denominational fund, administered by an anonymous clerk. Rather, it is one church sending a love gift to another, carried by their very own representatives.

16:4

"If it seems advisable for me to go also, they will accompany me."

Here Paul demonstrates his humility by being open to the advice of the local leadership at Corinth. Whilst he expects a letter from him to be enough to validate the offering, he is willing to listen to their counsel. However, his forthcoming apostolic visit to Corinth is part of an important wider itinerary. They would have to travel with him, at his pace, rather than go directly to Jerusalem. Paul's ministry is to establish and strengthen local churches, and also to remember the poor. If - for whatever reason - it would be advisable for the gift to travel with Paul, no doubt the Corinthian stewards would be greatly blessed to accompany him. To see firsthand his lifestyle, teachings and sufferings would surely be a privilege. Their father in Christ had many churches to care for; the Corinthian church was one of many in Macedonia, Asia and Galatia. Should these Corinthian brothers be required to journey with Paul, they would return with stories of hardship, faith, and breakthrough.

"Should these Corinthian brothers be required to journey with Paul, they would return with stories of hardship, faith, and breakthrough."

16:5

"After I go through Macedonia, I will come to you – for I will be going through Macedonia."

Acts 16 records Paul's second great missionary journey. At Troas (on the north west coast of Turkey) he had a vision of a man in Macedonia (part of modern-day Greece) standing and begging him to "come over and help us". Paul and his travelling companions concluded that God was calling them there to preach the gospel (Acts 16v8-10). Subsequently, Macedonia would no doubt have been a region close to Paul's heart. Macedonia was across the Aegean Sea from Turkey, and contained the great cities of Philippi, Thessalonica, and Berea on its coastal horseshoe. It proved open and responsive to the good news: the people received Paul's teaching, and churches had been established. This signalled the gospel first breaking out into mainland Europe. Now Paul plans to revisit the churches in Macedonia - but not as a train passes through a tunnel, rather as a stream passes through a desert, bringing life and strength.

> *"Now Paul plans to revisit the churches in Macedonia - but not as a train passes through a tunnel, rather as a stream passes through a desert, bringing life and strength."*

16:6

"Perhaps I will stay with you for a while, or even spend the winter, so that you can help me on my journey, wherever I go."

Paul presumes upon the hospitality of the Corinthians; this would have been normal, and he had already lived amongst them for 18 months. Travel in the first century was very dependant on weather. When Paul travelled to Rome, sent by Festus, his party considered spending the winter in Phoenix, Crete, because sailing had become dangerous (Acts 27v9). Paul saw Corinth as a safe haven, a place to stay for a season, not just to shelter from the weather but to spend time with this beloved church. He could rely upon them to provide for his own needs while he was with them, and to provision him when he moved on. Just as children should be quick to meet the needs of their parents, so Paul - as the Corinthians' father in Christ - presumes upon their desire to meet his needs. His next destination is as yet unclear even to him: "wherever I go" is best understood to mean "wherever the Spirit leads" (Acts 13v4, 16v6, 19v21, 20v22).

16:7

> *"For I do not want to see you now and make only a passing visit; I hope to spend some time with you, if the Lord permits."*

Knowing the state of the church at Corinth, and Paul's history and relationship with them, we can see how necessary it was for Paul to spend time there. There were deep factions in the church, and some animosity towards Paul (4v21). Written letters can only go so far in conveying love, truth and grace. Like all relationships, time spent face to face is time well spent. Prolonged togetherness is required. Paul did not want to make a passing visit, quickly pointing out shortfalls or issuing fleeting words of encouragement. He wanted to invest heavily in them, to spend several months or maybe a winter there, not just a few weeks. He would prefer to delay the visit if that helped to create time for a longer stay at a later date. For Paul a delay is preferable to a quick fix. And all of this is subject to God's will - not to Paul's schedule, nor the demands of the churches.

> *"Jesus was the true and greater firstfruits of the Festival of Harvest; his resurrected body revealed the quality and nature of the resurrection harvest to come."*

16:8

> *"But I will stay on at Ephesus until Pentecost,"*

Pentecost was a celebration marked by both Christians and Jews. Pentecost literally means 'fifty days', and for Jews it marked the time from the first Passover to the giving of the Law to Moses on Mount Sinai. It also became known as the Festival of Harvest (Exo 23v16, Lev 23v15-21). For Christians, the outline of the picture is the same but the meaning of the picture is so much richer. Jesus was the true and greater Passover lamb, who was slain to deliver God's people from God's judgement and slavery. And Jesus was the true and greater law-giver, in that His law is written not on stone tablets but on believers' hearts. Jesus was the true and greater firstfruits of the Festival of Harvest; his resurrected body revealed the quality and nature of the resurrection harvest to come. Paul wanted to stay on in Ephesus until Pentecost because there was work still to be done. Paul is about God's business and will come to the Corinthians in God's timing.

16:9

"because a great door for effective work has opened to me, and there are many who oppose me."

The advance of the Gospel and opposition to the Gospel were the two bookends to Paul's calling. When Paul first arrived in Corinth he preached in the synagogue every Sabbath trying to persuade Jews and Greeks. Eventually the Jews opposed him and became abusive. So he left there and went next door to the house of Titus Justus. Many Corinthians believed - including the synagogue ruler Crispus - and were baptised. But opposition grew. Jesus appeared to Paul in a vision, encouraging him: "Do not be afraid, keep on speaking...because I have many in this city" (Acts 18v1-22). The same pattern repeats in Ephesus, where Paul is writing this letter. He preached in the synagogue for three months but some there were obstinate, refused to believe, and publicly maligned the Way. So Paul used the lecture hall of Tyrannus for two years, hosting daily discussions. As a result he could write that all the Jews and Greeks who lived in the province of Asia (the coastal area of western Turkey) had heard the word of the Lord (Acts 19v10).

16:10

"When Timothy comes, see to it that he has nothing to fear while he is with you, for he is carrying on the work of the Lord, just as I am."

Timothy was Paul's travelling companion and delegate. We first hear of him in Acts 16v1. His mother was a believing Jewess and his father was Greek, and he lived in Lystra. The believers there spoke well of him, so Paul took him along. This began a fruitful gospel partnership of a spiritual father and son labouring together. It seems that Paul has already sent Timothy on his way to the Corinthians, or was planning to. Either way, Paul expected the letter to arrive before Timothy did. Paul asks the Corinthians to give him a warm reception; they would get more out of Timothy if they put him at ease. Timothy was a well-established delegate of Paul, albeit much younger, so it is likely that any animosity people had towards Paul would also be directed towards Timothy. So Paul reminds them that Timothy is about the Lord's work, not simply Paul's. Any argument they had against Paul or Timothy was also against the Lord.

> *"The advance of the Gospel and opposition to the Gospel were the two bookends to Paul's calling."*

16:11

*"No one, then, should treat him with contempt.
Send him on his way in peace so that he may
return to me. I am expecting him along with the
brothers."*

Timothy is more than a delegate of Paul; first and foremost he is about
the Lord's business. As such, no one should despise him (by writing this,
Paul obviously anticipates that some will). In this context Timothy needed
to stir up the gift within him and not let a spirit of timidity dominate his
visit! It was going to be a bumpy ride. It is worth noting that Paul was expecting Timothy to return along with 'the brothers': this suggests a group
of believers moving between the churches. These brothers were not nec-
essarily all men. Phoebe, a deaconess from the church in Cenchrea near
Corinth, is commended to the church in Rome (Rom 16v1-2). She was
presumably going from church to church encouraging, strengthening and
introducing new ideas. Priscilla and her husband travelled and equipped
churches and leaders in Rome, Corinth and Ephesus (Rom 16v3-4, Acts
18v 26, 1 Cor 16v19).

16:12

*"Now about our brother Apollos: I strongly urged
him to go to you with the brothers. He was quite
unwilling to go now, but he will go when he has
the opportunity."*

Apollos was well known to the Corinthian believers; some of them followed him as their preferred apostle (1v12). Apollos was Jewish and a
native of Alexandria, a learned man with a thorough knowledge of the
Scriptures. His theology had been helped by Priscilla and Aquilla. He
spoke with great fervour and accurately taught about Jesus (Acts 18v24-
25). He was a gifted but teachable follower of Jesus. Paul described Apollos as the one who watered the gospel seed that he had himself sowed
in Corinth (3v6). This verse is interesting if only because it gives us
an insight into apostolic tension. Paul strongly urged Apollos to visit
the Corinthians but he was unwilling - presumably he had other more
pressing work. But he does commit to visit them when he has an opportunity. Both Apollos and Paul labour in God's field: there is much work
to do, but God alone is the head gardener (3v5-9)! Note that Paul refers
to Apollos as a 'brother': this suggests a warm and affectionate relationship, not one of competition.

*"Timothy needed to stir up the gift within him
and not let a spirit of timidity dominate his
visit!"*

16:13 | *"Be on your guard; stand firm in the faith; be courageous; be strong."*

Here Paul uses the imagery of watchman and soldiers, calling the Corinthian believers to be vigilant in their faith. Their enemies are not warriors with swords but those who spread the false teaching that corrupts gospel truth and creates division. They have been set free from slavery to sin and the constraints of the Mosaic Law. They have been set free from idol worship and mere religious observance. Instead they are to stand firm in the grace of God, holding fast to the traditions taught by Paul, Apollos, Cephas, Timothy and the 'brothers' when they arrive (v10,12). The call to 'take courage' was a familiar refrain in Old Testament accounts of God's people facing overwhelming odds. Joab and Abishai declared this when fighting the Syrians and Ammonites in 2 Samuel 10v12. Likewise, Paul encouraged the Ephesians to 'be strong in the Lord and in the strength of His might' (Eph 6v10).

> *"The call to 'take courage' was a familiar refrain in Old Testament accounts of God's people facing overwhelming odds."*

16:14 | *"Do everything in love."*

The imagery of soldiers at battle and on guard is washed over with the motive of love. Not only is the use of spiritual gifts to be governed by love (chapter 13), but all the activities of life. Paul has already told the Corinthians what love looks like: Love never gives up. Love cares more for others than for self. Love doesn't want what it doesn't have. Love doesn't strut; Doesn't have a swelled head; Doesn't force itself on others; Isn't always "me first"; Doesn't fly off the handle; Doesn't keep score of the sins of others; Doesn't revel when others grovel; Takes pleasure in the flowering of truth; Puts up with anything; Trusts God always; Always looks for the best; Never looks back (The Message 13v4-8). Love will help the Corinthians to deal with disagreements, lawsuits, and immorality (1v10, 6v7, 5v5). Love must fuel their marriages and their singleness (7v5, 34). Love is to be the compass when navigating food sacrificed to idols and orderly worship (8v9, 14v26). The way of love requires courage, faith, strength and watchfulness. Given the difficulties within the church and the animosity towards Paul, this is more than a final parting platitude: it is a command, an exhortation, an imperative.

16:15

> *"You know that the household of Stephanas were the first converts in Achaia, and they have devoted themselves to the service of the Lord's people."*

Paul had arrived in Corinth by travelling west after leaving Athens and crossing the isthmus (the landbridge). By doing so he opened up a new region to the Gospel (Acts 18v1). Achaia is the body of land at the bottom of Greece, and was a Roman province. As Paul closes this letter, his thoughts turn to the founding members of the Corinthian church, the first converts in Achaia. Stephanas and his household seemed to have a special relationship with Paul. He baptised them and they imitated his life of service to the saints (1v16, 4v16). This household presumably watched and learnt from their father in Christ, and were clear fruit of his ministry. In Stephanas and his family the Corinthians had living local examples to follow, of those who faithfully believed and served God's purposes.

16:16

> *"I urge you, brothers and sisters, to submit to such people and to everyone who joins in the work and labours at it."*

Paul singles out Stephanas and members of his household for special mention. They had devoted themselves to the service of the saints - presumably this is a veiled reference to some form of leadership responsibility they held, as shepherds labour for the sheep. Either way, they were prominent enough to be mentioned at both the beginning of the letter (1v16) and its end. The believers in Corinth are urged to submit to them, just as Paul asks the Thessalonians to "respect those who labour among you and are over you in the Lord and admonish you" (1 Thess 5v12). The writer of the letter to the Hebrews puts it like this: "obey your leaders and submit to them, for they are keeping watch over your souls, as those who will have to give an account" (Heb 13v17). Note the warm relational language here: Paul addresses the Corinthians as his brothers and sisters, as fellow workers and labourers. Church relationships are to be to characterised by mutual love, respect and submission.

> *"Church relationships are to be to characterised by mutual love, respect and submission."*

16:17

"I was glad when Stephanas, Fortunatus and Achaicus arrived, because they have supplied what was lacking from you."

Most likely the three men Paul mentions here were established members of the Corinthian church, sent to Paul with the letter referred to in 7v1. Again we see the pattern of a group of delegates travelling between churches supplying Paul's needs. (In a subsequent letter to the Corinthians, Paul reminds them of the time when he was with them in Corinth but "brothers who came from Macedonia supplied my needs" - 2 Corinthians 11v9.) No doubt Stephanas, Fortunatus and Achaicus came with much needed news from the church in Corinth. But they brought more than just news. Stephanas would have been a source of great encouragement to Paul: he was the first fruit of Paul's ministry in that region, and Paul baptised his household (1v16, 16v15). The presence of these dear brothers causes Paul to feel the absence of the Corinthian's fellowship, love and support. They remind Paul of the deep sense of connection and partnership in the gospel he felt for the Corinthians.

> *"Believers are to use their God-given gift of encouragement to stimulate faith, rather than soothe or inflate egos."*

16:18

"For they refreshed my spirit and yours also. Such men deserve recognition."

Like everyone else, Paul's soul needed refreshing. The demands of life take a toll, even on those who follow Christ as best they're able. Stephanas, Fortunatus and Achaicus were the kind of people who were a joy to have around: their company revived you. These men devoted themselves to the service of the saints, leaving them refreshed, renewed, restored and revitalised. When they came to Paul carrying the church's letter, they were ideally qualified to be more than just a messenger. Paul often remarks on those who refreshed him: Philemon refreshed the hearts of the Saints; Paul hoped the Romans would refresh him; Titus was refreshed by the Corinthian church; Barnabas was a great encourager. The spiritual gift of encouragement (Rom 12v8) is highly valued by Paul, and it is easy to see why. Believers are to use their God-given gift of encouragement to stimulate faith, rather than soothe or inflate egos.

16:19

"*The churches in the province of Asia send you greetings. Aquila and Priscilla greet you warmly in the Lord, and so does the church that meets at their house.*"

The Roman province of Asia was the area we now call western Turkey: it is the connection between Asia and Europe. This area was key for trade and migration around the eastern Mediterranean Sea. Paul had travelled along this coast during his second journey and established churches there. He was clearly still in touch with these churches. It is worth reminding ourselves that "all the Jews and Greeks who lived in the province of Asia heard the word of the Lord" from Paul's time preaching in the Hall of Tyrannus in Ephesus (Acts 19v10).

Aquilla and Priscilla had fled from Rome to Corinth, where they first met Paul. They later moved to Ephesus, from where this letter was written. Now they send their greetings to the church in Corinth they helped to plant. They are involved in church life in Ephesus, hosting a congregation in their home. This was a time before churches had buildings. They would either hire a lecture hall or meet in someone's home, which - given the warm climate - could mean either indoors or in a courtyard.

> "*Commands such as this - to greet one another with a kiss - are best obeyed by understanding what the original readers understood it to convey.*"

16:20

"*All the brothers and sisters here send you greetings. Greet one another with a holy kiss.*"

Paul is writing from Ephesus, the other side of the Aegean Sea from Corinth. Yet despite the barrier of the sea, the Ephesian believers feel connected to their Corinthian brothers and sisters: they are joined through faith in Christ. Greeting one another with a kiss is still practiced in the Mediterranean. The original hearers would have understood this to mean greet one another warmly, with openness, in an unguarded manner. Given the factions and divisions amongst them, this command would be a significant challenge! This verse is relationally warm and calls for a demonstration of acceptance and unity. Commands such as this - to greet one another with a kiss - are best obeyed by understanding what the original readers understood it to convey. We need to be obedient and greet each other in a warm and unguarded way, in a way that demonstrates acceptance and unity.

16:21 | *"I, Paul, write this greeting in my own hand."*

It was not uncommon for Paul to write a personal greeting "in [his] own hand" at the end of a letter. At the end of the letter to the Colossians he writes a few brief words (Col 4v18), as he does at the end of his letter to the Philippians and his second letter to the Thessalonians. The picture here is of Paul dictating a letter to the church in Corinth, to which he then adds a handwritten personal greeting. Paul is not able to craft a letter as we would; he can't afford to draft and redraft it, because parchment was very expensive. So Paul has to first think about it, then he speaks his letter out and someone writes it down. This makes sense of the various digressions in the letter (1v16, 13v1-13). However, he wants this letter to be authoritative, so he writes a greeting in his own hand as "the distinguishing mark in all my letters" (2 Thess 3v17-18). When Paul dictated his letter to the church in Rome, his scribe Tertius also added a greeting to the church there (Rom 16v22).

16:22 | *"If anyone does not love the Lord, let that person be cursed! Come, Lord!"*

In this context, a curse is best thought of as an utterance intended to invoke God to inflict harm or punishment on a person, rather than a curse from witchcraft. Deuteronomy 11v26 records curses on God's people if they do not obey the commandment of the Lord. It was a serious pronouncement, not just a way of expressing frustration, anger or annoyance. To curse someone was to ask God to harm or punish them. What does Paul want the Corinthians to understand by this? Paul reminds these believers that a day is coming when the Lord will return. It will be a day of great blessing and terrible curses (6v9). In light of this coming day, Paul's hope is that believers would persevere and that many others would turn and follow Christ. This verse is Paul warning and encouraging the Corinthians to persevere in their faith and testimony for Christ. Jesus will come again, and that will be a great and terrible day. So it is highly appropriate to both long and pray for this day by declaring "Come, Lord".

> *"Paul is not able to craft a letter as we would; he can't afford to draft and redraft it, because parchment was very expensive."*

16:23 | *"The grace of the Lord Jesus be with you."*

Paul always thanked God for the grace given to believers. As he wrote at the beginning of his letter to the Corinthians, they had been enriched in every way (1v4). He concludes his letter with the same sentiment - only now he blesses them with ongoing grace and favour from God. They started with grace and he wants them to continue in it. They are not to compromise this grace by adding the observance of special days, months, seasons or years (Gal 4v10). Neither are they to cast off this grace by thinking that good works will gain their acceptance by God. They are to continue in the same grace they first received from God and continue to receive from Him. They are not to hope in their learning, wisdom, connections, spiritual gifts, sexual liberty or abstinence. Their identity, standing and confidence are all to be found in the grace given to them through their faith in Christ. They do not require the favour of apostles or civic leaders or teachers in their own congregation; they need only the grace of the Lord Jesus.

16:24 | *"My love to all of you in Christ Jesus. Amen."*

Paul started his letter by thanking God for the Corinthians (1v4) and he finishes it by expressing his love for them. Despite his reprimands and corrections and their opposition to him, his final word is of his love for them. Just as spiritual gifts need love as their motivation, so too is Paul's letter to this church motivated by love. Love in Christ is not self-seeking, nor does it keep a record of wrongs. Paul's love for these brothers and sisters compels him to write a letter of warmth and correction, a letter of encouragement and instruction. His final words - the lingering taste he wants to leave in their mouths - are of his love for them "in Christ Jesus". All those who have been called by God into fellowship with His Son (1v9) are to love one another as Christ loves us (John 13v34). Paul is not exempt from this command, and neither are we.

> *"Despite his reprimands and corrections and their opposition to him, his final word is of his love for them."*

72321004R00121

Made in the USA
Columbia, SC
19 June 2017